88 -

Praying the Passion of Christ

Uniting Your Suffering to His

Kathleen Beckman, LHS

D1372455

This book is presented in the form of the Spiritual Classic
The Imitation of Christ by Thomas A. Kempis

Queenship
PUBLISHING COMPANY
P.O. Box 220 • Goleta, CA 93116
(800) 647-9882 • (805) 692-0043 • Fax: (805) 967-5133

About the Author

Kathleen Beckman is a cradle Catholic, married 29 years and the mother of two sons. She is a *Lady of the Equestrian Order of the Knights and Ladies of Holy Sepulchre of Jerusalem* and the Coordinator of *Magnificat, A Ministry to Catholic Women,* for the Orange Diocese Chapter since 1992. She was nominated for the Orange Diocese Catholic Woman of the Year Award for her work at the *Lestonnac Free Medical Clinic.* She worked as a Medical Assistant for 14 years, then as co-owner of their family Lumber Business. Since the experience of a spiritual conversion in 1990, she is a daily Communicant and dedicates herself to a life of prayer and service in the Church. She is the leader of Intercessors of the Lamb Cenacle with three priests and has spoken at International Conferences on Conversion, Spiritual Warfare, and Prayer. She has penned 5 volumes of writings entitled; *I Will Restore You in Faith, Hope and Love.* She is a *Cursillista* and a frequent guest on St. Joseph's Catholic Radio.

Library of Congress Number # 2004106815

Published by:
    Queenship Publishing
    P.O. Box 220
    Goleta, CA 93116
    (800) 647-9882 • (805) 692-0043 • Fax: (805) 967-5133
    www.queenship.org

Printed in the United States of America

ISBN: 1-57918-261-5

Dedication

Dedicated to the Priesthood of Christ
Priests Who Taught Me the Science of the Cross

Fr. Raymond Skonezny, STL, SSL, Spiritual Advisor since 1992

The late Fr. Richard Foley, SJ
(Farmstreet Church, London, England)

Fr. Larry Darnel, OMI

Fr. Michael Philen, CMF

Fr. Joseph Droessler

✝ ✝ ✝

O Lord, bless them as they have blessed me.
Daily they feed me the Bread of Life,
They cleanse my soul in the Sacrament of Mercy,
They conferred Baptism, Confirmation, and Marriage,
They anoint my sick relatives and bury the dead,
Encourage me along the Via Dolorosa,
Counsel me with wisdom and patience.

For the sake of all families and nations,
Daily they offer Sacrifice in Your Holy Name,
Commit themselves to prayer and service,
Devote their time to selfless works of mercy,
Lead the flock in the Truth of Salvation,
These priests live Your Perfect Sacrifice.

Dear priests of Jesus, the Christ,
The Lord shares His Passion with you.
Hold fast to the promise of resurrection.
Your crown awaits you in His Courts.
Persevere to lay down your lives for the Church.
Drink deeply of His Eternal Love and live.
Receive the gratitude of the Body of Christ.

Acknowledgements

I gratefully acknowledge those who have helped in the
preparation of this book and ask the Lord's
blessing upon you and your families.

Mrs. Marilyn Hollingsworth,
thank you for typing the manuscript
and gift of your precious time.

Fr. Raymond Skonezny,
thank you for writing the Foreward and your
patient advice as my spiritual director.

Fr. Michael Philen,
thank you for writing the Preface
and your priestly intercessory prayer.

Fr. Joseph Droessler,
thank you for praying me through some difficult times.

Thank you, United Hearts of Jesus and Mary Cenacle,
for your prayerful intercession and discernment.

Mrs. Karen Moses,
my prayer partner and life long friend, thank you
for always being available to my family and me.

Mrs. Donna Ross,
my mentor and prayer partner, thank you
for your example of fidelity to God.

Bob, Claire, and David Schaefer at Queenship Publishing,
thank you for your kind support, advice
and dedication in publishing this book.

To my family,
thank you for teaching me the way of sacrificial love.

Table of Contents

From the Author

Fulton J. Sheen wrote, "Some books are written to answer one's own questions; other books are written to question answers already given. This book was written to find solace in the Cross of Christ, as for about ten years of my life, I endured a great trial. The nature of that trial is not important, but what is important is how it was met."
(Preface: *The Life of Christ* by **Fulton J. Sheen**).

The prayers and meditations in this book are the fruit of a long period of tribulation in my life. I know that all people suffer and at one time or another, each person will be backed up against the wood of the Cross. Then Christ Crucified will be your solace and the Cross your intimate friend.

The grace of my spiritual conversion in 1990 brought me back to the Church, the Sacraments and prayer. I received a revelation of the Lord's Divine Love as I began to open my heart in prayer, especially through the Eucharist, the rosary and Baptism in the Holy Spirit. My life would never be the same. The fascination I had with worldly ambitions became a fascination with the Christ Crucified though I knew little of suffering.

Then quite suddenly a cross came into our family that would break my heart open and push our family to the edge. Where did I run? To Calvary! To whom would I go to find solace and wisdom? To Christ Crucified! My life was backed up against the cross and I had a choice to run from it or to remain on Calvary's Summit.

By the grace of God, I chose Calvary's Summit and tried to live, one day at a time, the kind of Sacrificial Love that Christ Crucified exemplifies as He hung on the Cross. Not that I wanted to be a victim but that I chose to love like Christ. The Passion became my consolation and the Cross, my school of love. I could do nothing in the midst of such pain but surrender to God's Permissive Will and remain faithful to the Lord's Law of Love.

Over time, after many tears, dark nights and tests of faith. . . I let go and let God. Suddenly, my joy returned and I was free again. My situation did not change but I had changed. I became a new creation by embracing the Cross for love of God because I was healed of my selfish love.

Uniting my sufferings to His is the practice of co-redeeming with Him and the foundation of intercessory prayer. The Apostle Paul clearly defines this teaching of co-redemption. In 12 years of ministry in the Church, I discovered a need for better understanding about the meaning and value of suffering on earth. If the science of the Cross is not understood, it breeds anger, rebellion, unforgiveness, and bitterness in personal suffering that touches humanity. May this book be a little tool in the hands of those whose lives are backed up to the wood of the cross. Prayer has the power to change me, the Church Militant, and the world in turmoil. I have witnessed the transforming power of praying the Passion of Christ, uniting my suffering to His!

The book is presented in the dialogue style of the Spiritual Classic: *The Imitation of Christ* by **Thomas A. Kempis**

Foreword

Fr. Raymond Skonezny, STL, SSL

I highly recommend this book, *Praying the Passion of Christ, Uniting Your Suffering to His*. The laity, religious and priests alike will find it a rich source of material for private meditation and spiritual reading. The reader will come away with a deeper insight into the meaning of the Christian Life.

It calls to mind the words of St. Theresa of Lisieux placed at the beginning of Part Four in the Catechism of the Catholic Church. (#2258) Under the question of "What is prayer?" the Church cites her words, "For me, prayer is a surge of the heart; it is a simple look turned towards heaven, it is a cry of recognition and of love, embracing both trial and joy."

Truly the prayers and meditations presented to us arise from a surge of a prayerful heart. Kathleen's life is prayer that has been formed by the Lord in His Passion. It is in the union of her heart with that of Christ Crucified that brings forth the wellspring of inspiration present in this volume.

In a dialogue form Jesus speaks to His disciple and the disciple responds in the style of the *Imitation of Christ* by Thomas A. Kempis. From the Cross Jesus speaks to those who suffer. It is to Him that the disciple brings our questions, our pleas for understanding the value in all human suffering. His response to our prayer is the words He spoke to His disciples, "Follow Me." It is in that following even to the Cross that we discover the Salvific Love present in suffering with The Lord.

In the prayers of the Saints throughout the ages we see revealed the mystery of their union with Christ's Passion. The Apostolic letter of Pope John Paul II, On the Christian Meaning of Human Suffering (Salvifici Doloris #26) has a very poignant passage, "The Divine Redeemer wishes to penetrate the soul of every sufferer through the heart of His Holy Mother, the first and most exalted of the Redeemed." In the meditative prayer entitled "Mary's Passion" we see these words of the Holy Father strikingly illuminated. From there to the grieving mothers of today Jesus enters their hearts through the sorrowing heart of His Mother.

Through the experiences of her personal Calvary and countless hours of prayer, Kathleen touches us with an insight, spiritual wisdom and grasp of the heart of our faith in Christ. The Lord has taught her to see the great lesson that the Cross brings to us: through that Cross Jesus has conquered the death that sin brought into our world. To suffer in Christ out of love is the disciples' lot. Through it the disciple lives. In it is found interior peace and spiritual joy. It is the surrender to Love Incarnate hanging on the Cross that makes us a light to the world and the salt of the earth.

The prayers we find in this work reveal how suffering strips the soul of the self and prepares it for the inrush of grace. The Holy Spirit, the Sanctifier, the One Whom Jesus sends to us, enlightens our mind and gives us the courage to embrace this Cross. In this embrace the author has lived for years and discovered that in every tribulation, "The Shade of His Hand outstretched caressingly".

Such a soul can say with St. Paul, "Now I rejoice in my sufferings for your sake and in my flesh I complete what is lacking in Christ's afflictions for the sake of His Body that is the Church." (Col. 1:24)

Ultimately, the meditations bring to us this mystery of the Cross. It is present in the lives of all those who have had the Cross traced on their foreheads at their Baptism. The Church, the Body of Christ, throughout all of time bears the marks of this suffering. The various meditations of this work are a testimony of this reality.

A hymn in the Priest's breviary comes to mind. One of the stanzas reveals the underlying value of all suffering for the servants of the Lord: "Take up your cross and follow Christ, nor think till death to lay it down; for only he who bears the cross may hope to wear the glorious crown." These words slide smoothly over our lips but it is only when they come crashing into our hearts that the cost of being a Christ bearer can be accepted. All suffering in Him carries the hope that He crowns us with His life and love forever.

Our author, who is a wife and mother, has discovered joy in the sacrificial love required in both vocations. The scope and intensity of her sacrifice have produced in her a union with Christ

Crucified that radiates authentic Christian joy. From the vantage point of the Cross she views with Christ's eyes the world of suffering. It is to Him that she invites us all to come and pray because it was there she found her consolation and hope.

May these inspired meditations and prayers help you to carry your daily crosses and bring forth fruit a hundredfold. Disciple, find solace in the Cross of Christ!

Fr. Raymond Skonezny, STL, SSL.
Spiritual Director

Preface

Fr. Michael Philen, CMF

I am honored to share these words with you on *Praying the Passion of Christ: Uniting Your Suffering to His*. There is a line from William Blake that says: "We are put on this earth for a little space that we may learn to bear the beams of love." Christ bore "the beams of love" for us, and He calls each of us to follow Him by the narrow way of the Cross. For the Christian, this is a noble and heartrending call—to follow in the footsteps of the Lord—to participate in His passion, death and resurrection. Kathleen Beckman has heard and accepted this call to discipleship. She is a woman of faith and action, a true disciple of the Lord. Since her conversion, she too has "learn(ed) to bear the beams of love". She has willingly and lovingly taken up her cross and followed the Crucified Christ to the Glory of His Resurrection—where He makes "all things new".

Praying the Passion of Christ: Uniting Your Suffering to His is a call to discipleship and draws the reader into a personal encounter with our Crucified Savior and Lord and His Holy Mother Mary. The book takes the form of a dialogical meditation—a teacher/disciple relationship—on the Passion of Christ. It enkindles our heartfelt devotion to Christ and veneration of His Mother. We relive the Passion with them and through their Hearts. It is "devotional" in the true sense of the word; it calls for complete surrender to God. "Devotion" in the root sense of the word, means consecration—the giving of oneself totally to God, our Loving Father. It involves a graced decision and commitment to the Lord that permeates our lives, giving direction and grace to all our actions through the Power of the Spirit at work within us.

This book calls each of us to make a decision for Christ <u>now</u>, because tomorrow may be too late! Do we want to be forgiven and transformed by Love Itself? Hurry! Let us run to meet the Savior. Where will we find Him? Look! He is hanging on the Cross, the Tree of Life, for all to see, waiting patiently for us; because a crucified Savior cannot run. Love Itself has been crucified for us. What is our response? We are called to be devoted disciples of the Lord in good times and in hard times. Jesus never promised to take away all our suffering, but He promised not to abandon us and He is faithful to His promise. His Life-giving Spirit dwells within us. We have seen His faithfulness and give thanks.

Fr. Michael Philen, CMF

Prayer: O Man of Sorrows,
May I Comfort You?

O Saving Victim, may I soothe your wounds?
Your Passion moves my heart, may I love like You?
O Holocaust for sin, may I be an offering too?
O Sacrificial Lamb, will you lift me?
Cover me with your Precious Blood?

May I drink water gushing from your pierced side?
May I be a balm for your deepest wounds?
Be a bandage for your Bleeding Body?
May I take a thorn from your Crown?
Take a nail from your hands or feet?

May I give You a drink of my love,
Though it is a just a little stream?
May I be a lamb like You?
Kiss the Cross for love of You?
See the Eternal Good of this Act of Love?

May I be the one who returns to thank You?
When darkness descends, the earth quakes, thunder roars,
When the veil is rent, may I still embrace the Cross?
May I trust in its saving grace?
O Lord, May I console You, Jesus of Nazareth?

May I be like Abraham who believed?
Job who persevered?
Esther and Ruth who did your bidding?
May I be like John the Baptist, who prepared the way for You?
Like Paul, full of zeal? Like Peter, a rock?

May I be like Simon of Cyrene, Veronica, Magdalene,
John the Beloved?

May I be like your Holy Mother?
May I stand with You forever?
Will you share your garments of purity?
May I hide inside your Holy Wounds?
Explore the caverns of your Heart?

May I enter Love's silent chamber?
Will the door open to your castle, mystical house?
May I enter and approach You like a beggar?
Will You have pity and sup with me?
O Living Host, may I be like you?

May I be poured out for love of You?
Until I breathe my last, may I breathe for You?
Count all things as rubbish except for You?
Forever, may I adore You!
O Saving Victim of Perfect Love!

O Man of Sorrows may I comfort You?
My Redeemer, may I imitate You?
Through your Passion may I radiate your Love?
My King, May I serve You in humility?
Let it be, O August Sacrament, if it please You!

✞
Prayer: O Holy Cross!

O Holy Cross, how much you have taught me! How necessary that I die a thousand deaths to overcome attachments, faults, vanities and pride. O Holy Cross, teacher of the Truth, pierced by your Light, I see the reality of my human nature, so weak and sinful.

O Holy Cross by your crushing I have been recreated. I will praise you forever! You gave birth to wisdom in me by putting to death my pride. You have woven a garment of humility for me. My shame is covered in your robe of mercy. You broke my rebellion and made me obedient to the law of love. You showed me the way to exchange the lie I was living for the Truth of the Gospel. I became lowly and you raised me up.

O Holy Cross, I tried to reject you repeatedly. I tried so often to run away from the pain. But Truth pursued me and would not leave me alone. O Holy Cross, I did not appreciate you in the beginning. You stripped away all my defenses and made me vulnerable to love's dependence upon Divine Providence. Praise you, O God, for this Holy Cross!

O Holy Cross, you worked a wonder in my little soul. You broke open my heart and purified my love. Your weight crushed my sins and independence. Grace flooded my soul through the diminishment you brought into my daily life. I had to choose: you or I? My hands were empty. There was no choice to make. O Holy Cross, I chose you! No matter the cost, I chose you!

I praise you, Father, Son and Holy Spirit for the holy cross that you chose for me! For love of You, I surrender unto its transforming power. Be glorified, My God!

Meditation:
Mothers at the Foot of the Cross

The Lord

Mothers, behold your Holy Mother at the foot of the Cross. See how she stands courageously embracing the Divine Will of the Father. See how she encourages her Only Son to complete the mission of redemption. Her eyes are filled with tears of compassion. She desires to suffer with Me and surrender in totality to My Sacrifice of Love. She knows I must pay the price to ransom Mankind and wills it. Her heart is suffering the anguish particular to mothers who observe their offspring, their own flesh and blood, suffer torment of every kind.

Mothers, place yourselves beside her at the foot of the Cross and learn. Emulate the Virgin Mary and she will impart maternal wisdom and fortitude in your sufferings. Let the Immaculate Mother be your consolation in the midst of your maternal heartaches. She will show you the way to offer sacrifice and prayer for your loved ones, for your children suffering from illnesses and sinful choices that separate them from you, the family, and the Church. Surrender your children unto Me and unite yourselves to Mary at the foot of the Cross. Unite to My passion and become part of My sacrifice. Remember that your children are not beyond My reach. My Arm is Almighty and I am more than able to reach them no matter where they wander. Become patient with your offspring, willing to wait for My Grace to flood their souls. Entrust them to Me. See My Sacrifice at Calvary as a testimony of My endless love for children, for all my offspring.

Disciple

Lord, I will do as You ask but such trust in You requires special grace. My children are flesh of my flesh, woven in the fabric of my maternal heart. The bond that I feel with them surpasses my understanding. This gift of motherhood is yet a mystery to me that unfolds daily. The burden I carry for my children is born of a love that is incomprehensible to me. Lord, help me to love unconditionally, without selfish ambition. Grant that I do not expect them to be a mirror of myself. Bless my motherhood with Your infused gift of Wisdom.

The Lord

Look to Mary Immaculate! Place your hearts into her Immaculate Heart and she will become your healing medicine and maternal milk. She will impart her own strength and move you to prayer and selfless love for your children. She is the Mother of the unceasing prayer, your Co-Redemptrix, Mediatrix and Advocate.

Mothers, love your children unconditionally so as not to cause them to lose heart. Be a vessel of hope for a future that is bright. Impart My Perfect Love to them so they see My Face in yours. Live your faith in Me with joy so they may see your happiness and freedom in Me. Then they will be moved toward Me. If you doubt, they will mirror your doubt. If you are afraid, they will become paralyzed by fear. If you forgive, they will learn mercy and be healed.

Mothers, you draw grace upon your children and families. Do not underestimate your power to effect change through love and prayer. Through Holy Communion I become your strength and Wisdom is imparted. Pray the rosary from your heart and your heart will enlarge to become more loving, more like our Holy Mother. Walk the Via Dolorosa with Me and suffer your children to come unto Me. My Blood covers all. Have hope!

Disciple

O Lord, I surrender my children unto your Merciful Love. I unite my children to your Passion and place them in your Holy Wounds. O Lord, I await in trust, the grace of conversion for my children. I believe that you will reach them and rescue them from the spirit of the world. O Lord, Savior of the world, it is not for me to save them. Only you can save them. You have already done so! Have mercy upon our children and the offense given to You. From the Cross, You said, *"Father, forgive them for they know not what they do"*. Grant that I, too, may forgive them. Grant that I may forgive myself also for the imperfection of my maternal love.

O Lord, in this day and age, the little ones seem so lost and confused. Grant that they may be found and healed. Gather them unto your Sacred Heart. Let the flames of your Divine Love purify this generation. Wash the little ones clean as snow and bring them back into healed families and a healed Church. May your Eucharistic Love, the Sacrifice of the Mass, draw them like a magnet. Reveal your love for them through me and through the Church. Grant them hunger for True Life in You and thirst for Your Precious Blood.

O Lord, by the power of the Holy Spirit, sanctify our children and consecrate them in the Truth. I believe that You are able to pierce and break open their hearts. Holy Spirit, come with your fire! Release your Divine Light to overcome the darkness that entangles so many of our children. Jesus, I trust in You. Amen.

Meditation: The Triumph of the Cross

The triumph of the Cross
Victory looks like defeat
Sin is crucified on the wood.
Death becomes passage to life.
Flesh of the Lamb is sacrificed.
The spirit of the world is overcome.

The Spirit of Love is poured out.
Precious Blood flows for new life.
The Head bows in humility.
The Body, the Church, is born.
The Pierced Heart baptizes creation.
Divine Love sets free the captives.

Wisdom confounds the enemy.
Garments divided, the veil is rent.
Earth shakes, the skies darken.
It is finished, it has begun!
Fire of Love redeems creation.
One ransomed all!

Christ claims His family back!
Obedience is the only way.
One Blood Sacrifice for all time!
Five wounds perpetuate the Truth.
Perfect Love is undefeatable!
The Father's Divine Will prevails!

Calvary is Love's Foundation.
Whoever goes to Calvary is blessed!
Blessed to gaze upon Virtue and Beatitude!
Blessed to be covered in Blood and Water!
Blessed to unite with the Lamb of God!

Blessed to become the Lamb's image!

The Lamb's Heart is Love's Fountain.
Mother Mary rests in the Heart of the Lamb.
The Two hearts are one, pierced at Calvary.
Whoever is one with the Two Hearts,
Is pierced mystically and born anew!
This Mystery is repeated in His Offering.

Whoever embraces the Cross, triumphs!
Enter the Mystery of God's Infinite Love,
Incomprehensible condescension!
Only a lamb can go there.
There is no shame in suffering in this life.
The Word Made Flesh sets the example.

To lay down one's life for another is to live!
To be fully human is to be Christ!
Love's victory exists in every moment.
The gates of hell cannot defeat His Victory.
Whoever kisses the wood, embraces Truth,
Lives forever in the glory of Divine Love!

This is the Triumph of the Cross!

✝
Meditation: Calvary's Summit of Love

The Lord

Perfect Love compelled Me to save you, to pay the ransom, to drink the cup, so that I was poured out for the sake of every person. I was raised up on the wood, hanging between heaven and earth that I would draw all things to Myself to the glory of The Father and for salvation of the world. I bore your sins on My back. I carried your needs in My Heart. By My stripes you are healed. I became sin so you would be free. I willed to die so you would live. What hymn of gratitude do you offer? What victory song do you sing? Is your heart moved by My Love? Does My Passion stir you to compassion?

Disciple

Lord Jesus, Savior and victim for my sins, I have failed to respond to your perfect love throughout my life. Often I am blinded by selfish love and worldly attitudes. There are moments of grace when I am moved by your Passion and my heart is uplifted at the sight of the crucifix. For a moment I appreciate the gift of my salvation and utter a brief prayer of gratitude, a sigh of affection for your Sacrifice. Then quickly I return to the duties of my vocation without further thought of You. Change my heart, O God, and have mercy upon me.

The Lord

I tell you the truth that I offered My Body as a holocaust in expiation of your sins because of the love I have for you. This bitter Passion is the revelation of Perfect Charity. From the cross I said, "I thirst". It is for you that I thirst. Do not hesitate to come to Me! My Heart is always inviting. Do not lock Me outside of your life. Welcome My friendship! You are hungry for love and I alone can satisfy your hunger. Allow Me to speak the Truth to your heart and show you the path that will lead to your Eternal Homeland.

I am your Savior King and My Kingdom is for you. Why

throw away eternal riches for the passing things of the world that satisfy your heart for only a moment in time? Acknowledge your emptiness and powerlessness. Forsake the way of self- sufficiency and take hold of My Almighty Hand. I am Sovereign. Surrender in faith. Place your hope in Me. Give Me to drink of your love.

Disciple

My Redeemer, I desire to surrender my heart in totality. I want to experience Divine Charity and become like You, full of love! My Lord, take my little hand into your Almighty Hand and walk with me through this valley of tears. Train my ear to your Voice. Fill my loneliness with Your Presence, my ignorance with Wisdom. Change my selfishness into generosity and service for others. Give me to see your Holy Face smiling upon my lowliness. May I see myself only through your merciful eyes and come to the realization that I am a child of the Most High God. Heal my many wounds and broken heart. Nurse me back to wellness. Augment my little faith that seeks many signs. Let me rest in the Silence of unseen Eternal Realities. Purify my heart, cluttered with base longings and lift me to Calvary's summit of Love. Teacher, instruct your pupil. Amen.

Meditation:
The First Word of Jesus on the Cross

Quote: **Anne Catherine Emmerich**

The countenance and whole Body of Jesus became even more colorless. He appeared to be on the point of fainting, and Gesmas, the wicked thief, exclaimed, *"The demon by whom he is possessed is about to leave him."* A soldier then took a sponge, filled it with vinegar, put it on a reed, and presented it to Jesus, who appeared to drink. *"If thou art the King of the Jews"*, said the soldier, *"save Thyself, coming down from the Cross."* These things took place during the time that the first band of soldiers was being relieved by that of Abenadar.

Jesus raised his head a little and said, *"Father, forgive them, for they know not what they do."* And Gemas cried out, *"If thou art the Christ, save Thyself and us."* Dismas, the good thief, was silent, but he was deeply moved at the prayer of Jesus for this enemies. When Mary heard the voice of her Son, unable to restrain herself, she rushed forward, followed by John, Salome, and Mary of Cleophas, and approached the Cross, which the kind-hearted centurion did not prevent. The prayers of Jesus obtained for the good thief a most powerful grace; he suddenly remembered that it was Jesus and Mary who had cured him of leprosy in his childhood, and he exclaimed in a loud and clear voice, *"How can you insult Him when he prays for you? He has been silent, and suffered all your outrages with patience; he is truly a Prophet—he is our King - he is the Son of God!"* This unexpected reproof from the lips of a miserable malefactor who was dying on a cross caused a tremendous commotion among the spectators; they gathered up stones, and wished to throw them at Him; but the centurion Abenadar would not allow it.

The Blessed Virgin was much comforted and strengthened by the prayer of Jesus, and Dismas said to Gesmas, who was still blaspheming Jesus, *"Neither dost thou fear God, seeing thou art under* the same condemnation. And we indeed justly, for we receive the due regard of our deeds; but this man hath done no evil. Remember thou art now at the point of death, and repent." He was enlightened and touched: he confessed his sins to Jesus, and said, "Lord, if thou condemn me it will be with justice." And Jesus replied, "Thou shalt experience my mercy." Dismas, filled with the most perfect contrition, began instantly to thank God for the great graces he had received, and to reflect over the manifold sins of his past life. All these events took place between twelve and the half-hour shortly after the crucifixion; but such a surprising change had taken place in the appearance of nature during that time as to astonish the beholders and fill their minds with awe and terror.

Quote: *The Dolorous Passion of Our Lord Jesus Christ*
by **Anne Catherine Emmerich**
Tan Publishers, 1983, pages. 280, 281

Prayer: To Forgive Like Christ

O Lord, in the midst of your agony on the Cross, You prayed: *"Father, forgive them, for they know not what they do."* Grant that I too, may forgive from my heart all those who have hurt me in any way. May the roots of unforgiveness be pulled from the soil of my heart so they do not become the weeds that choke my ability to love and be loved. I have been deeply hurt and disappointed in my own family and friends, even people in the Church. I desire the grace to pray blessings upon those who persecute me and intercede for those who maltreat me. Lord, please heal my hypersensitivity so that I am not so easily offended by others words or opinions.

Lord, how often I withhold mercy towards others. How burdened I am with hurts from long ago, painful memories that occupy a place in my heart where there could be grace and mercy. What harm I am doing to myself and to You when I refuse to let go of the memories, the injuries, the unloving words and deeds that keep me from being completely free. I pray to be set free of these chains now.

Lord, I desire to forgive myself, also, that I may be set free from any warped self image or distorted view of the person You created in me. Allow me to see myself through Your eyes only and recognize my identity and dignity in You. Help me to care for my body, mind, and soul as a temple of your Holy Spirit. Help me, Lord, to believe that I am wonderfully made and precious in Your sight. By the mercy I receive from You, I shall become a vessel of mercy. I surrender all of the injuries of my past, present and future unto Your Divine Mercy. Grant that I may become healed from unforgiveness and become a dispenser of Your Mercy. Amen.

Prayer: The Father's Loving Sacrifice

O Father of the Word Incarnate,
It is written: God is Love.
In your mercy, You sent Your only begotten Son.
He became the testimony of Your Covenant.
Man sinned and paradise was lost.
You willed to save man, to open heaven.
You willed it and the Word became flesh.
He dwelt among us, the Light in the darkness.
He came to His own but His own did not receive Him.
He spoke only of You and proclaimed Your Kingdom.
He bore witness to Your perfect Goodness.
He mirrored your Beauty, reflecting Your Face.
He put aside His Majesty and became lowly.
He fled from riches and became poor.
He shunned His power and took on weakness.

O Father of the Sacrifice,
The spotless Lamb bore our iniquities.
Clothed in garments of rejection and mockery,
He was misunderstood, betrayed and crucified.
His Blood poured out and water gushed from His side.
He gave birth to the Church through His pierced Heart.

O Eternal Father, He glorified You in obedience.
And You glorified Him extending Your Kingship.
Your Covenant of Eternal Love is written.
Your Seat of Mercy is the Word Incarnate.
Your Only Begotten Son, Jesus,
The Christ said from the Cross, "It is finished."
Redemption is accomplished, salvation won.

O Heavenly Father, still You await our fiat.
The cloak of His Precious Blood, the robes of Royalty,

Enfold us only as we will it and surrender.
We must open the door of our hearts.

O Father, Wise and Omnipotent Love!
Shower my heart with mercy and grace.
Melt my stubbornness, rebellion, and selfishness.
Pierce my darkness and annihilate my sin.
Let the Sword of the Spirit, your Word,
Break my resistance and cowardice.
Let the flames of your Eternal Love envelop my heart.
Turn stone into Living Water.
Consecrate my heart in the Truth.
Save me from my self and the world.
Draw me to your Light.
Change me into His Image.
Write His signature all over my heart.
Cause me to love like Him!
Breathe His Passion into my life.
Affix my will to the Cross that saves.
Satisfy my thirst for Love,
Then pour me out for others.

O Father, Sovereign and Ineffable Love,
Look at me, so lowly a creature,
See the dust that I am and have pity!
Ransomed by the Blood of the Lamb,
Pick me up into your Almighty Arms,
Embrace me as Your offspring.
Let me glorify Your Holy Name!
Abba, Father be glorified in your little victim of Love.

O Father, eternal, creative, and dynamic Love!
Speak anew the life and power of His Holy Wounds,
Cleanse the earth by His Precious Blood.
Perpetuate His Passion, Death and Resurrection.
Until the end of all ages, let there be Light!
Let the Victorious Lamb reign on earth as in heaven. Amen.

Meditation: Can You Drink The Cup?

Disciple

Heavenly Father, I offer my life, my will, joys, and sufferings on this earth in union with the passion of Your Son, His Precious Blood, and Holy Wounds in reparation for the atrocities of this generation.

Father, have mercy on me and on the whole world. Indifference, pride, vanity, and rebellion cause us to reject Jesus still. We crucify Christ Jesus repeatedly. Where we should unite and love, we divide and fail to love. Almighty God, convert our hearts and infuse the light of Truth. Banish the evil that entices us to darkness and sin. Renew our faith in You.

Eternal Father, open wide, the floodgates of Divine Mercy. Rescue Your people from the present crisis of love. May the Good Shepherd manifest His Divine Charity to revive His Bride, the Church. May the Holy Spirit change the world and restore holiness. Father, Your will be done on earth as in heaven.

If you are searching for someone to sacrifice for others, receive my soul as a holocaust for sinners. Father, grant me the grace of complete submission to Your Divine Will. Let Charity reign in my soul and use me for Your glory. Keep my sacrifice hidden for Your eyes only. Humble me daily. In secret fashion me into the image of the Suffering Servant. May I drink the cup for love of You?

The Father

Disciple, do you know what you are asking? Can you drink the cup of suffering to become the image of the Suffering Servant, the mirror of the Lamb who was sacrificed? Do you think you are capable of such generosity of the heart, mind, and body? You are weakness through and through! Yet I have planted this desire into your heart and patiently awaited the moment when this seed, that I planted, would sprout life in you. I will pour Living Water into the fallow soil of your soul to bring forth this seed of desire for union with My Son. I will lead you to Calvary and instruct your heart so that you grow in Wisdom. In due season, you will see that I chose you from the beginning to bear good fruit for My Kingdom. As you grow daily into the image of your Savior, you will beautify the Church and draw many souls unto My House. Your prayers will have power before My Throne, because you are robed in His Garment of Blood. I accept your offer born of My Paternal desire.

Meditation on the Sorrowful Mysteries

Disciple

O Lord, from the Garden of Gethsemane to Calvary, I watch You suffer for me. In every stage of your agony, I see myself and many familiar faces. It is this present generation who is carrying out your Crucifixion.

The Lord
The Garden of Gethsemane:

Through My blood filled eyes, yours were the faces I observed, yours were the sins I bore in My Body and Spirit. From the beginning of time I knew you and saw what your generation would become, a sin-sick generation. In Gethsemane I saw your faces as terror shook my Body and Soul. My capillaries burst and I sweated blood for love of you. In the midst of that dark night of man's betrayal, I trembled for your sake. In a moment of extreme desolation, I asked My Father that this cup would pass by. In obedience I united My will to His and surrendered myself up for you.

Scourging

This generation scourges Me again. Like an animal I am bound and bent over a pillar to expose my back to the whip. Flesh is torn apart from My bones. Blood and flesh fall to the ground. The whip in your hands is formed of sins of pride, greed, hatred, idolatry, anger, and lust. Wayward generation, do you know your sickness? Are there any among you who know the meaning of sacrifice? Will you come to repentance now? If you expect Mercy, wash yourselves in the Blood that spills from My Body. Behold the Lamb of God who is sacrificed.

Crown of Thorns

You have crowned Me with mockery. Your lips profess that I am your King but your actions reveal that you have made yourselves god. Your Savior sees everything you do in secret. Humble yourselves and surrender unto My Kingship. Thorns pierce My Sacred Head and the throbbing pain is excruciating. You are there in the crowd when Pilate offered to let Me go and you joined with the others and said, "Crucify Him!"

Carrying the Cross

Behold the sign of contradiction, the Cross of crucifixion! I walk the Via Dolorosa with two common theives. You are there in the crowd staring. Are you moved to sympathy? Are you indifferent like most of those observing the horror of this spectacle? See the capacity for violence that exists in the depths of the human heart? I stumble and fall three times. Are you willing to stand close to Me and acknowledge that you know Me now? Or do you hide yourself among the jeering crowd and deny Me again? Are you close enough to see that I am looking at you and loving you?

Death on the Cross

Behold the Man! Do you hear my gasping for air as I prayed to the Father: *"Forgive them, for they know not what they do."*? When I struggle to breathe and utter the words *"I thirst"*, are you close enough to take it in? Do you observe what little flesh hangs on my bones? Do you see My eyes fixed on you even through the blood-ied, matted hair? Do you know that Pure Love is communicating from His Pierced Heart? Do you see that I have made myself vulnerable to all of creation? I saw you as I hung between heaven and earth, raised high upon the Cross. I knew you from the beginning of all ages and willed you to be with Me forever. I have paid the price for you. Console your Savior.

Disciple

All glory and praise be yours, Lord, Jesus! Have pity on me, a sinner. I am sorry for my offenses and the indifference of this generation. I beg Your pardon and mercy upon creation. By the eternal merits of Your Passion, I beg mercy. Your cup of justice is full, but You command the Angel of Justice to delay the trumpet to gather more souls unto Yourself. Merciful Love is the fountain of grace to convert the world from sin to sanctity. You saw our faces in the midst of Your agony and understood that we scorned You through ignorance and fear. Engrave in my heart the sign of the Cross. May I recall and reverence Your sacrifice all the days of my life. May all souls be drawn into Your perpetual outpouring by means of the Holy Cross and receive the grace of Resurrection.

Prayer: O Passion of Christ!

O Passion of Christ, consecrate my heart.
Anoint Love's fervor all over my life.
Create ardent desire to perpetuate your sacrifice.
That I live now not for myself, but only for You!

O Passion of Christ, become my praise,
And hymn of perfect charity.
Be my fragrance of purity and joy.
Lift my spirit into your own.
That I may breathe Love's Truth,
And augment your Sanctuary.

O Passion of Christ, unite me to Calvary.
Open my eyes to see the Glory.
Wrap my arms around the Cross.
Incline my ears to your Pierced Heart.
Let the rhythm of Sacrificial Love resound in me.

O Passion of Christ, transfigure me!
Crucify my wayward spirit.
Create something new and beautiful.
Yours is the power to transform!
Change the sinner in me.
Let holiness become my covering.
The horror and shame of your death,
The scandal of the Cross,
Became eternal victory and glory!
You confounded the cunning Enemy,
Opened heaven's gate! Carry me there!
Through your Wounds, may I enter?

O Passion of Christ, engrave my soul!
Let Divine Love reign in my life.

Teach me of holy victimhood.
That I may die to self and rise in YOU!
Through your Wounds, I find my true identity.
In Your loving Sacrifice I gain freedom.
You lead the way to live fully,
The Gospel of Life and Your Law of Love

Meditation: Carrying the Heavy Cross

Disciple

I see the scene unfold on the small, winding street of the Via Dolorosa. I see Jesus bent over, physically exhausted, and struggling with the weight of the Cross. O what a terrible sight! The Lord of the universe, the Spotless Lamb, carrying the weight of sin!

I see Simon of Cyrene pulled from the crowd and made to assist Him because Jesus was nearly collapsing. I see Veronica wipe the sorrowful Face of The Lord. Many jeered at her for doing so. Her loving courage was rewarded by Jesus, who left His Image on the cloth.

I see Our Lady together with the Beloved Apostle John. Our Lady is full of Light in the midst of union with the sufferings of the Lamb. Her Radiance, seen by Jesus, strengthens Him. I see the eyes of Jesus and the Beloved John lock in a loving gaze that speaks volumes. I understand that John absorbed every detail of this awesome moment into the depths his heart: He watched, pondered, prayed, and suffered as if he understood he would one day make a full account.

I saw Mary Magdalene close to Mother Mary and John; her sorrowful, tender heart was torn asunder to see Him suffer this horror. These people, Simon of Cyrene, Veronica, Mary Magdalene, the disciple John and Mother Mary are the ones I see nearest the Lord as He carries the Cross.

The Lord

Simon of Cyrene represents you who come to Me with small faith, who approach Me with fear, who seek Me half-heartedly and for your sake not Mine. See, I do not send you away. I take your small effort and pour Grace upon you. I say, *"Do not be afraid. Give Me your hand and I will bless you."*

Veronica represents you who step out in faith, who have courage to leave what is safe and comfortable to come to Me; you have compassion for Me and want to serve Me. I reward your humble service. My Image is on your heart. I say, *"Come close to My Holy Face and see the expression of Divine Love for you. My eyes tell of My desire for you."*

Mary Magdalene represents every converted sinner whose heart blazes with love. I turn your poverty into the richness of Divine Life. I turn your self-indulgence into self-sacrifice. I turn your pride into humility. I lavish My tender forgiving love upon you. You have gratitude and become willing to sacrifice everything for Me. I say, *"Once you were apart from Me, lost in the world, but now you have experienced My Love, let us rejoice."*

John, the beloved disciple, represents you who are faithful disciples, beginning to end. You draw close to My Sacred Heart. Lean on My love. You desire to be taught by Wisdom and soar to the heights of love. You remain faithful in the midst of every difficult trial. You are another beloved disciple and great will be your reward.

To every one, I say, *"Behold your Mother."* Take her as your own. Allow her to teach and guide you to become a faithful disciple of these trying times. Listen to her maternal wisdom. Ponder everything in your heart. Then Light will shine in the darkness of your age. You are the salt of the earth. Great will be your reward in heaven. My Vicar, John Paul II, is such a disciple.

Mother Mary represents the dignity of every man, woman, and child on earth. Her maternal heart embraces all of creation. Full of the Holy Spirit, she is your beacon and pillar of courage. I said to her, *"Behold your Son."* Since the utterance of these words, her Obedient Heart has never ceased to behold and cherish, nourish and pray, suffer and intercede on your behalf. Blessed are you who, *"Behold your Mother."* Every good and necessary grace will be yours through her Immaculate Heart. There are many levels of discipleship from Simon of Cyrene to the Virgin Mother and she is the summit of discipleship.

Meditation: Mary's Passion

Mother of the Lamb, Masterpiece of the Trinity.
Your flesh is unblemished, perfectly sustained in Grace.
Still, you suffered the Passion as the sword pierced your heart.
Yours was an unspeakable interior and mystical union.
Your Two Hearts are as one living pulse of love poured out.
You willed that He complete His Redemptive Mission.
Urging Him to undergo the Suffering, you were His signpost.

He saw in you His own desire to obey the Father's Will.
He observed your courage when His flesh was spent.
He saw your flesh radiant with love when torture enveloped.
He willed to comfort you but you encouraged Love's Sacrifice.

When He said, "This is your son," you became the Mother of John,
You became the mother of the human family.
Your Son was the key to the future and hope of all men.

When heaven offered consolation at Calvary, you willed only to suffer.
You drank the cup with the One Born of your Virginal flesh.
Mother of Christ Crucified, you were crucified too.
Not in the flesh but in the depths of your maternal heart.
Your tears of compassion washed the face of the human family
So that man would be cleansed from defilement and receive redemption.

When the Redeemer expired and gave up His Spirit,
You remained to give hope to His disciples.
In trembling they walked away while you remained courageous.
You and John and Magdalene embraced the Sacrifice of the Lamb.

On Easter Sunday the Glorified Body of Christ appeared to you.
His Resurrected Glory permeated your Immaculate being.
Your joy was complete but your mission was not.
He ascended to the Father and you remained with His apostles.

Mother of the Church, you aided her beginning, laying a foundation.
With Maternal Wisdom and Solicitude, you taught the disciples.
Your instruction was fruitful, your prayers fulfilled.
The Mystical Body of Jesus was formed in the Light of your Love.

There in the Upper Room they gathered around you in prayer.
The Mother of the Redeemer led the way to Pentecost.
Spouse of the Holy Spirit, you drew the Grace of His Visitation.
As you desired, He descended upon the one hundred and twenty.
The Church came to life on that day of empowerment.

Mother, grant us the grace to imitate your Art of Love.
Mother Immaculate, teach us the Science of the Cross.
Mother of Christ Crucified, teach us the value of redemptive suffering.
Bring human suffering into the light of truth; make fruitful our tears.

Mother of the Lamb Sacrificed, lead us out of selfish love.
United to Jesus, guide us to co-redeem with Him and gather souls.
He sanctified the human condition of suffering and wrapped it in glory.
Pray for us, O Mother, that we know the value of suffering with Christ.
Pray for us, O Mother, that we embrace our cross and live in Him.
Pray for us, O Mother that we may participate in Love's Sacrifice.

Mother Mary

Beloved disciple, the crucifix is a school of Divine Love. Enter into its teaching often. Permit your heart to enter this sign of contradiction and you will grow in the knowledge of God. Enter freely into the greatest act of Divine Love. His Passion is a gift for you. Your little crosses must be seen in the proper perspective so that you do not lose heart. Never hesitate to draw close to the sufferings of my Son, our Savior. Many people avoid the teaching of the Cross because they do not understand unconditional love and mercy. People fear to contemplate the mystery of God's Love because it may touch them personally and intimately. Such an outpouring of Perfect Charity demands a response, does it not? Too few want to respond to the revelation of the Mercy of God, the outpouring of His Divine Heart. Beloved disciple, you are blessed to respond. His Light will lead you from glory to glory. You will walk in the security of salvation and receive peace.

Meditation: The Priest Victim

O Lord, bless your Priesthood.
You are the One Eternal High Priest.
Your Victimhood is perpetuated
In those chosen men, ordained priests,
Set apart for You and the Church.

O that they would know
The dignity of their calling!
When Your people look upon them
O Lord, let us see Your Holy Face;
The countenance of Your pure light.

May their eyes reflect Your Perfect Love.
Their hearts beat in rhythm with Your Heart,
Their holy hands extend Your Healing Touch,
Their voices speak your Word with authority.
This brotherhood perpetuates Your Sacrifice.

In this age when they are attacked,
Move to separate the wheat from the chaff,
Separate the goats from the sheep.
Renew them in Your Perpetual Love.
Anoint them with the Oil of Gladness.

O Lord, stir up zeal for Your House,
Courage for spiritual warfare!
Confer Wisdom upon your priests.
Gather them unto Your Kingly Heart
Teach them of their Royalty in You.

O Jesus, send Virgin Mary to aid them.
O Immaculate Heart, Mother of God,
Nourish the priesthood with maternal milk.

Reveal the glory of the Thrice Holy One
Strengthen contemplation and service.

Unite them to the Lamb of God,
Along the Via Dolorosa walk with them
By means of your maternal love,
Ever gentle, patient and wise,
Bless the priesthood of the Lord.

O Spouse of the Holy Spirit,
May the Radiance of the Spirit issue forth,
Envelop the chosen brotherhood of Priests.
Raise them to heights of unity and love,
Open the floodgates of Mercy
Restore and heal your priests!

Meditation:
Could there be Any Greater Love?

The Lord

The Word became flesh and dwelt among you. I am your Deliverer and King! I purchased you by My Blood and you belong to Me. I am with you. You are My temples, offspring, and seed. I am hidden in the humble species of Bread so that you do not fear to approach Me. Come to Me! Approach Me without fear! I know you are searching for Me, for your Father, and the Holy Spirit. You are looking also for your Holy Mother! You have need of God, of your Mother Mary, too! Your needs are known to Me. You thirst for love and need a sign of My affection for you. In the Eucharist, Holy Communion, I impart My Resurrected Glory into your hearts.

When you need a sign of My True Love, look intently upon the Crucifix. Draw close to My Pierced Side and drink of Love's outpouring. Place yourself close to My Passion and you will receive consolation. Hide yourselves in My Wounds and you will understand that I died so you would have life. Could there be any greater Love? Are you afraid to draw closer to My Passion? Are you afraid to receive My Sacrifice of Love? Are you afraid to be changed into the Suffering Servant?

Come, beloved! Draw close to your Savior! You are lonely and in need of Divine Companionship. Make yourselves available to Me and I will be your constant Friend. Ask the Holy Spirit to teach you the art of loving. Perfect Love casts out fear! When you love more perfectly, when you experience My Love more fully, your fears will change into steadfast, expectant faith.

Let go, My beloved disciples! Let go of your self sufficiency and depend only on Me. Do not look to man for the love and security that comes only from God. The Thrice Holy One will provide for you. I will never forsake you! Believe in My covenant promises! Contemplate My Sacrifice of Love. Embrace the cross without fear. I am trustworthy and cannot lie.

Disciple

O Lord, I am afraid to be changed into the suffering servant. I am afraid to draw closer to Your Passion, because I do not have perfect love. You see that my spirit is willing, but my flesh is weak. Only you can change the weakness of my humanity into the courage of the saints and the martyrs. These holy ones were mere humans also. What changed them so thoroughly? How did they embrace the cross so readily and display such stupendous courage in the face of martyrdom? Is it not a matter of Your Grace being more than sufficient to supply for every need and circumstance?

O Lord, grant me the grace to become fearless in the face of suffering. Grant that I may love as You love and become willing to lay down my life so others may live in You. Augment my weak faith; let it become the mustard seed so that I may move mountains to bring souls to You. Change me so thoroughly that I become Your Face in the crowd, Your heart in my family, Your Spirit in the Church. I believe that all things are possible in and through you. Still, help my unbelief, Lord. Change my love of comfort and desire for transient things into love of spiritual realities, desire for sanctity, and zeal for Your House. Grant that I may draw close to your Cross and see the value of my suffering in this world, keeping my eyes fixed on the world that is to come. Let me boast in nothing except the Cross and You Crucified. Jesus, I trust in you. Amen.

Meditation:
In the Name of Christ Crucified

Quote: **Catherine of Siena**

"I have shown you, dearest daughter that in this life guilt is not atoned for by any suffering simply as suffering, but rather by suffering borne with desire, love, and contrition of heart. The value is not in the suffering but in the soul's desire. Likewise, neither desire nor any other virtue has value or life except through my only-begotten Son, Christ crucified, since the soul has drawn love from Him and in virtue follows his footsteps. In this way and in no other is suffering of value. It satisfies for sin, then, with gentle unitive love born from the sweet knowledge of my goodness and from the bitterness and contrition the heart finds in the knowledge of itself and its own sins. Such knowledge gives birth to hatred and contempt for sin and for the soul's selfish sensuality, whence she considers herself worthy of punishment and unworthy of reward.

So you see, said Gentle Truth, those who have heartfelt contrition, love for true patience, and that true humility which considers oneself worthy of punishment and unworthy of reward suffer with patience and so make atonement.

You ask me for suffering to atone for the offenses my creatures commit against me. And you ask for the will to know and love me, Supreme Truth. Here is the way, if you would come to perfect knowledge and enjoyment of me, Eternal Life: Never leave the knowledge of yourself. Then, put down as you are in the valley of humility you will know me in yourself, and from this knowledge you will draw all that you need.

No virtue can have life in it except from charity, and charity is nursed and mothered by humility. You will find humility in the knowledge of yourself when you see that even your own existence comes not from yourself but from me, for I loved you before you came into being. And in my unspeakable love for you I will to create you anew in grace. So I washed you and made you a new creation in the blood that my only-begotten Son poured out with such burning love.

This blood gives you knowledge of the Truth when knowledge of yourself leads you to shed the cloud of selfish love. There is no other way to know the truth. In so knowing me the souls catches fire with unspeakable love, which in turn brings continual pain. Indeed, because she has known my truth as well as her own and her neighbor's ingratitude and blindness, the soul suffers intolerably. Still, this is not a pain that troubles or shrivels up the soul. On the contrary, it makes her grow fat, for she suffers because she loves me, nor would she suffer if she did not love me.

Thus, as soon as you and my other servants come in this way to know my truth you will, for the glory and praise of my Name, have to endure great trials, insults, and reproaches in word and in deed, even to the point of death. Behave, then, you and my other servants, with true patience, with sorrow for sin and love of virtue, for the glory and praise of my name. If you do, I shall be appeased for your sins and those of my other servants. The sufferings you endure will, through the power of charity, suffice to win both atonement and reward for you and for others. For you they will win the fruit of life. The stains of your foolishness will be blotted out, and I will no longer remember that you had ever offended me. As for others, because of your loving charity, I will pardon them in proportion to their receptiveness."

Quote: *Catherine of Siena: The Dialogue*
by **Suzanne Noffke, O.P.**
Paulist Press, New York, 1980, pages.29, 30

Prayer: The Church in Her Agony

Holy Mother Church, You hold a Treasury.
The Treasury of Faith handed down,
From Jesus to Peter to Pope John Paul II,
House of God, Born of His Pierced Side,
Fountain of Grace Issuing from His Heart
One, Holy, Catholic, and Apostolic,
River of Life, Foundation of Truth,
In every age, you suffer too,
The passion of Christ, your Head!

The Mystical Body of Christ
Lives in the light of the Resurrection.
Still the Agony of the Garden lives in you,
The Scourging at the Pillar continues,
The Crown of Thorns surrounds you,
Daily you carry the cross up the hill.
To Calvary you ascend and are pierced
Broken open and spilled out
For every woman, child and man!

Church Crucified is Church Alive!
Racked by tension, you grow!
Tried and assaulted you get stronger!
Blood of the Lamb, blood of the martyrs,
Co-mingle and becomes your Ocean
And the Ship that you are continues
To sail through every storm
Anchored in the Truth of
Love's Incorruptibility!

And the gates of hell that come against
Shall never prevail upon you as

The perpetual sacrifice of Jesus, the Christ,
Is daily lived out on Your Holy Altar!
His Heart beats in His Mystical Body,
His Breath gives Life to Her members,
His Sacraments augment His Bride
Your Sanctuary is secure to the end of time
The Word is written and it is true.

The Lamb of God draws us to His House
He is the Door that opens wide
To beckon all to come to Him
He adorns His Mystical Bride
With Unspeakable Beauty and
Fragrances Her with Sanctity that
Comes from the Thrice Holy One!

He invites us to become little lambs
Following the way of the Cross,
Familiar with Calvary's Sacrifice.
He asks that we daily deny ourselves,
Take up our Crosses and follow Him.
Where does He lead us?
To Calvary that we may live,
To His Pierced Heart of Mercy!
Raised high upon the Wood
We embrace His Self Immolation
And find ourselves healed there
In His Wounds of Love!

Torrents of Grace overcome us
And we are moved to glorify Him.
We cannot love Christ, the Head,
And cease to love the Body of Christ.
Together, they live and move in unity.
Holy Mother Church, Minister of God's Love
Continuation of His Eternal Priesthood,
I offer myself to you, as a servant,

Victim of Sacrificial Love!
Grant that I may be an obedient child
Leaning on your Wisdom from on High
Not upon my own human understanding!
May I never walk apart from your ranks
But forever embrace you as Holy Mother Church
And endless Baptismal Fount of Life!

Meditation: The Wounds of a Marriage

Disciple

O Lord, when in my youth, I approached your Holy Altar in the Church and your priest joined us, man and woman, two became one in Your Heart. In the springtime of our union, all my dreams seemed fulfilled and we put our arms around one another in the goal of pursuing Your Divine Will that we become a family, a domestic Church, bringing forth the fruit of love. After many seasons of satisfaction and joy, many years of working sacrifice, a wedge was driven into our union and the words "I do not love you anymore" pinned me to the Cross.

When I was thus pierced and my heart torn asunder by another's choice, when I had no control to fix the situation and had to surrender everything unto Your Mercy, You gave me a place to put my unspeakable pain, the Cross of Calvary. In the midst of the torment of my own crucifixion, I found comfort there in Your Holy Wounds. My tears would flow in self pity until I looked beyond my cross to see Your Passion in the light of true love. There I learned that love is a sacrifice, a call to lay down my life for another. There I learned to drink the cup and rely on You for everything.

As I gazed upon the Crucifix, I saw Eternal Promise and value of suffering united to Your Cross. I understood the Church's Teachings. You taught me to focus on the salvation of our souls. In this exile on earth my expectations of this marriage have fallen short. You ask me to look beyond this valley of tears to an eternal life in the Father's Kingdom where there are no more tears.

I came to understand that one day in Your Courts is better than a thousand elsewhere. You taught me love's sacrifice and collected my tears to water the family with blessing. In obedience, I followed your commands and You healed my wounds. I know now the joy of the Cross and the true meaning of a sacrament of love. It is quite possible to love without being loved in return. I came to appreciate being chosen to suffer this and have gained everything by this cross. I praise you, O Lord, for teaching me of Your Passion through my sacramental covenant. It led me to Calvary's victory over sin and crushed my selfish love.

The Lord

On that day of your wedding, I stood before you in the person of the Priest. My Sacred Heart opened wide to embrace you and your spouse, so very young and eager to embark on your own journey. My Love poured out in blessing then and throughout the many years of fruitful love. I blessed you with children born of love and welcomed into a true family. There were many seasons of light and joy and very little suffering at all. For a time, you became forgetful of Me. But I would never forsake your family. For a time, work and wealth became your goal and the busy-ness of your lives allowed little time together. But I would never forsake your family.

When the spirit of the world came against your union, the grace of the sacrament sustained your family. You were compromised but held together even if only by a string. This string is the thread of grace issuing from the rope that binds a marriage in God. Such a string is not a means of constraint but a means of freedom from error, freedom from selfish love, unabashed immorality. These are the ties that bind the human heart by enslaving it to carnal passions. The carnal person will perish by the flesh. The flesh crucified brings forth the spiritual person and eternal life.

Your sacrifice, your sacrament, forms a crown of glory for you, a ring of eternal love that shall become your joy in your true homeland. The privations of the flesh on earth unleash a torrent of divine grace into the soul and raises up holy men and women of wisdom and godly virtue. You become the radiance of Divine Love and walk in healing grace to forge a path of charity that is a light to the world.

Your vision of the marriage was not fulfilled because of human weakness and sin. My Precious Blood becomes your covering and by My Stripes, you are healed. Who gave the grace to forgive? Whose tenderness melted away your bitterness? I came to you with My Sacred Heart in My Hand and provided grace in your time of great need. I supply for all your needs. Your sacrament is a fountain of divine grace. My Passion becomes your place of refuge and hope. Love draws you there. I will never forsake your family. Suffer the family unto Me.

Meditation:
The Stigmata of St. Francis of Assisi

Then one morning about the Feast of the Exaltation of the Cross, as he was praying on the mountainside, Francis saw a Seraph with six fiery wings coming down from the highest point in heaven. The vision descended swiftly and came to rest in mid-air quite near him; then he saw that the Seraph was nailed to a cross although he had wings.

Then Christ who appeared to him visibly, granted him spiritual enlightenment. It was set before his eyes that, as Christ's lover, he might know he was to resemble Christ Crucified perfectly, not by physical martyrdom, but by the fervor of his spirit. As the vision disappeared, after they had conversed mysteriously in great intimacy, it left his heart ablaze with seraphic eagerness and marked his body with the visible likeness of the Crucified. It was as if the fire of love had first penetrated his whole being, so that the likeness of Christ might be impressed upon it like a seal.

There and then the marks of nails began to appear in his hands and feet, the heads of which were in the palms of his hands and on the instep of each foot, while the points protruded on the opposite side. The heads appeared black and round in his hands and feet, but the points were long and bent back; they rose above the surrounding flesh and jutted out above it. The curved portion of the nails on the soles of his feet was so big and stood out so far that he could not put his feet firmly on the ground; a man could put his finger through the loop without difficulty, as I have been told by people who saw the stigmata with their own eyes. His right side was marked with a livid scar which often bled, and it looked as if it had been pierced with a lance. His habit and trousers used to be soaked with blood, so that the friars who washed them knew at once that Christ's servant bore the likeness of the Crucified in his side, just as he bore it in his hands and feet.

Full of God as he was, Francis realized that he could not possibly conceal from his intimate companions, the stigmata which had been imprinted so plainly on his body. At the same time, he was afraid to make God's secret publicly known and he was thrown into an agony of doubt—should he reveal what he had seen, or keep silent about it. His conscience was pricking him and he eventually gave a full account of the vision, although very hesitantly, to the friars who were closest to him. He told them, too, that Christ had revealed a number of secrets to him, at the time of the apparition, which he would never communicate to any human being, as long as he lived. True love of Christ had now transformed his lover into his image, and when the forty days which he had intended spending in solitude on the mountain were over and the feast of St. Michael the Archangel had come, St. Francis came down from the mountain. With him he bore a representation of Christ Crucified which was not the work of an artist in wood or stone; it had been inscribed on the members of his body by the Hand of the living God."

Quote: *Omnibus of Sources: St. Francis of Assisi,
Minor Life by **St. Bonaventure***, pages 821, 822, 823.
Franciscan Press, Quincy College, December 5, 1972

Meditation: Betrayal of the Lord

Disciple

Lord, I can see You in the Garden of Gethsemane. You had already heard the footsteps of the soldiers coming to arrest You so You were standing up. Your heart quickened in anticipation of the betrayal. You suffered not anxiously but peacefully because of Your obedience and surrender. Your time had come and You willed this baptism to redeem sinners but this did not reduce Your agony.

I can see Judas and the band of soldiers approach You, Lord. Peter, James, and John stood with You in silent anticipation. You imparted strength to Your apostles but they had fear in their hearts and Peter was ready to fight. I observed closely how Judas came near to You and kissed You on the cheek.

You are betrayed by a sign of affection that is meant to express love. How much You loved the apostle Judas! This added to Your suffering. At that moment of betrayal, I see Your Heart pierced with sorrow for Judas. I see Judas' heart at that moment too. It was wrenched in contradiction.

After the kiss of betrayal and a short conversation to identify the Nazarene, the soldiers apprehended You. You offered no resistance but Peter could not contain himself and raised his sword to the ear of one of the soldiers. You reprimanded Peter. Then You were taken to a place of detention. It was underground and made of rock.

Before You were put into the cell for the night, bound by Your hands and feet, the soldiers took turns buffeting Your Face. I see continuous blows to Your Face and Head in slow motion and hear the laughter of those who torment You. I see the clenched fist of the soldier repeatedly strike with full force. In the midst of such a beating Your peaceful Countenance remains. The agony is obvious but the focus is on the loving composure of Your Holy Face, the power of Love.

The Lord

Disciple, never despair! When, in weakness you fall to sin, I am near to extend My Hand, to pick you up, and offer the cup of forgiveness. Never run away from Me like Judas and hide yourself in despair. Your life is not your own to give up. In the darkness of your confusion and chaos, in the moment of realization of your sinful deed, I reach out for you. Never fear to reach for My Almighty Hand.

All men sin and every sin is a betrayal of Love's truth. But I have already paid the price for your sins and purchased for you, the gift of forgiveness, the Mercy of the Father. Come to the Fount of Divine Mercy and be washed in the Salvific Blood of your Savior.

Yes, sinful disciple! I am your personal Savior. I suffered and died and rose again for the sake of every individual person! You are known to Me and more precious than gold. I do not require human perfection: only that you allow yourself to enter into the Perfection of the Great I AM. This is a process of purification and sanctification that leads to transforming union. Paradise is filled with sinners who were perfected in the Fire of Divine Love.

Do not become discouraged when you fall. Know that when you betray Me by sinning, you war against your true self, betraying your own dignity! My Heart is tender and I am moved to help you regain your footing and begin again along the narrow and steep way of your daily cross. No matter how severely you repeatedly buffet My Face, if you look closely, you will see My Eyes of Mercy upon you. These Eyes of Love beckon you to return to yourself and come unto Mercy's Holy Face. Disciple, never despair!

Meditation:
St. Paul: Co-Redeeming with Christ

St. Paul's physical sufferings began after his dramatic conversion experience. He was temporarily blinded (Acts 9:8) and deprived of food for three days (Acts 9:9). The Jews sought to end his life, and his own disciples were afraid of him (Acts 9:23-26). By the age of sixty years, Paul had been for more than ten years engaged in the harshest of missionary works and endured ruthless beatings from mobs, all for the sake of following Christ Jesus. The Apostle's own description of his anguish at this time is recorded in 2Cor.11:24-30.

"Five times I have received at the hands of the Jews the forty less one. Three times I have been beaten with rods; once I was stoned. Three times I have been shipwrecked; a night and day I have been adrift at sea; on frequent journeys, in danger from rivers, danger from robbers, danger from my own people, danger from Gentiles, danger in the city, danger in the wilderness, danger at sea, danger from false brethren; in toil and hardship, through many a sleepless night, in hunger and thirst, often without food, in cold and exposure. And, apart from other things, there is daily pressure upon me of my anxiety for all the Churches. If I boast, I will boast of the things that show my weakness."

This beloved apostle teaches suffering from an entirely different level. "The present trial is a slight momentary affliction and it is preparing for us an eternal weight of glory beyond all comparison." (2Cor.4:17) "We may be afflicted in every way, but not crushed." (2Cor.4:8)

Paul further warns of the inevitable encounter with the evil one and teaches us to prepare for it: "Put on the whole armor of God that you may be able to stand firm against the tactics of the devil. For our struggle is not with flesh and blood, but with the principalities, with the powers, with the world rulers of this present darkness, with the evil spirits in the heavens." (Eph. 6:11-12)

Paul becomes a victim of God's love and sharer in His unending Passion. He desires to help carry our burdens (Gal. 6:2) and does so voluntarily: "I will most gladly spend and be spent for your souls." (2Cor.12:15). The Apostle encourages everyone to offer their sufferings to God for the sake of sinners: "Do not yield your members to sin as instruments of wickedness, but yield yourselves to God as men who have been brought from death to life, and your members to God as instruments of righteousness." (Rom. 6:13) "I appeal to you therefore, brethren, by the mercies of God, to present your bodies as a living sacrifice, holy and acceptable to God, which is your spiritual worship." (Rom. 12:1)

Paul offers himself up voluntarily and unconditionally to atone for sinners, and becomes one specially marked by God to be His victim for others, "Now I rejoice in my sufferings for your sake, and in my flesh I complete what is lacking in Christ's afflictions for the sake of His Body, that is the Church." (Col. 1:24) "Even if I am to be poured as a libation upon the sacrificial offerings of your faith, I am glad and rejoice with you all." (Phil. 2:17) "Now I rejoice in my sufferings for your sake." (Col. 1:24) Paul wanted to be transformed into another Christ crucified, as he himself so clearly states, "that I may know him and the power of his resurrection, and may share his sufferings, becoming like him in his death... ." (Phil. 3:10) "I bear in my body the marks of Jesus Christ." (Gal. 6:17)

Prayer to St. Paul for Courage

Apostle Paul, victim of God's love, united to the Passion of Christ, intercede for me that I may not fear to suffer my cross and do so with great generosity and steadfast confidence in the saving grace of the Blood of the Lamb. Assist me, Apostle Paul, to endure the hardships of life with complete abandonment to Divine Providence. Pray for me, that I count the things of this world as nothing and boast only in Christ Crucified. Teach me the way of co-redeeming, the way of sacrificial charity and undefeatable zeal for souls. Pray for me that I may become a victim of Divine Love and deemed worthy to lay down my life so others will live in Jesus, the Christ. I pray through your powerful intercession, for the grace to rejoice in my sufferings for the sake of souls and to the glory of God. Shroud my weakness in your strength and zeal. Amen.

Meditation:
The Agony in the Garden of Gethsemane

O Desolate Garden!
Utter darkness of night
O night of agony
Drowning in sorrow
Piercing isolation
O weight of the world
Sin so deadly
Humanity so fleeting
Death so promising

O tortuous sacrifice
O silent suffering
Resounding stillness of night
Chill penetrating My bones
Heart abandoned, body trembling
Blood and sweat dripping
Have you forsaken Me, Father?
Take this cup from me
Not Mine, but Your will be done.

O sin of all ages
Bearing down upon Me
Obedience overcoming disobedience
Love overcoming everything!
Wind that whispers torture
Death unlike any other
Surrender, my soul, surrender!

O Father, the hour has come
Glorify Me that I glorify You
Eternal life be purchased

I pay the blood ransom
Receive my offering eternally
Now all shall have life

O darkness of this lonely night
Cover the lonely darkness of man
Love agony cancels man's sin
O how I love, I love, I love
Alone I am, alone I am not.
I will drink the cup!

Meditation:
His Wounds Spoke of God's Love, Padre Pio

By His Holiness Pope John Paul II

A Man of Prayer and Suffering: In 60 years of religious life, practically all spent at San Giovanni Rotondo, he was totally dedicated to prayer and to the ministry of reconciliation and spiritual direction. This was well emphasized by the Servant of God, Pope Paul VI: "Look what fans he had . . . But why? . . . Because he said Mass humbly, heard confessions from dawn to dark and was…the one who bore the wounds of our Lord. He was a man of prayer and suffering." (Feb. 20, 1971).

Totally absorbed in God, always bearing the marks of Jesus' Passion in his body, he was bread broken for men and women starving for God the Father's forgiveness. His stigmata, like those of Francis of Assisi, were the work and sign of divine mercy, which redeemed the world by the Cross of Jesus Christ. Those open, bleeding wounds spoke of God's love for everyone, especially for those sick in body and spirit.

And what can be said of his life, an endless spiritual combat, sustained by the weapons of prayer, centered on the sacred daily acts of Confession and Mass? Holy Mass was the heart of his whole day, the almost anxious concern of all his hours, his moment of closest communion with Jesus, Priest and Victim. He felt called to share in Christ's agony, an agony which continues until the end of the world.

Dear friends, in our time, when we are still under the illusion that conflicts can be resolved by violence and superior strength, and frequently give in to the temptation to abuse the force of arms; Padre Pio repeats what he once said: What a dreadful thing war is! In every person wounded in the flesh, there is Jesus suffering!

As for the prayer groups, he wanted them to be like beacons of light and love in the world. He longed for many souls to join him in prayer: *"Pray"*, he used to say, *"pray to the Lord with me, because the whole world needs prayers."* And every day, when your heart especially feels the loneliness of life, pray, pray to the Lord together, because God too needs our prayers!

It was his intention to create an army of praying people who would be a "leaven" in the world by the strength of prayer. And today the whole Church is grateful to him for this precious legacy, admires the holiness of her son and invites everyone to follow his example.

Quote: The homily was taken from the English and Italian editions of *L'Osservatore Romano,* May, 1999, The Beautification of Blessed Padre Pio in Rome.

Prayer: St. Faustina's Act of Oblation

Jesus Host, whom I have this very moment received into my heart, through this union with You I offer myself to the heavenly Father as a sacrificial host, abandoning myself totally and completely to the most merciful and holy will of my God. From today onward, Your Will, Lord, is my food. Take my whole being; dispose of me as You please. Whatever Your fatherly Hand gives me, I will accept with submission, peace, and joy. I fear nothing, no matter in what direction You lead me; helped by Your grace I will carry out everything You demand of me. I no longer fear any of your inspirations nor do I probe anxiously to see where they will lead me. Lead me, O God, along whatever roads You please; I have placed all my trust in Your will which is, for me, love and mercy itself.

O Jesus, stretched out upon the Cross, I implore You, give me the grace of doing the faithfully the most Holy Will of Your Father, in all things, always and everywhere. And when the will of God will seem to me very harsh and difficult to fulfill, then I beg you, Jesus, may power and strength flow upon me from Your Wounds, and may my lips keep repeating, *"Your will be done, O Lord"*.

O Savior of the world, Lover of man's salvation, who in such terrible torment and pain forget Yourself to compassionate Jesus, grant me the grace to forget myself that I may live totally for souls, helping You in the work of salvation, according to the most Holy Will of Your Father. Amen.

Quote: *Diary of **St. Faustina Kowalska**,* pages 456, 457
Association of Marian Helpers, Stockbridge, Mass., 1966

Prayer: Considering Your Passion, Death and Resurrection

My Jesus, this Holy Week, after considering your Passion, Death, and Resurrection, the love You have for me and the extent of Your mercy, I wish to renew my "Act of Oblation" to My Savior and King.

When I was in darkness, You breathed on me, reviving me from spiritual deadness. You bent from heaven with the revelation of Your Love. Suddenly everything became vanity except You! You freed me when I never knew I was bound in chains. You saw that I had made myself the master of my life. I was like a sheep without a shepherd, wandering on my own path. You saw I was in danger, perishing daily in independence. Love compelled You to rescue me. You conquered my stubbornness and suddenly I knew My God! In knowing You, I discovered myself. Order was restored to my life.

Your Love ignited a fire within my heart that has never ceased to burn intensely. The flames of Love consumes me. In the beginning, You wooed me away from the world, filling me with consolation. Then You baptized me by fire. I suffered many tests of faith but grace carried me. You moved quickly through my heart asking for more love and sacrifice, virtue and service, and more transformation into You.

You led me to Calvary, the place of transformation. I am on the Cross with You now. In the midst of this suffering, I choose You again. Nothing the world offers compares to Your companionship. I will live and die in You. Your Precepts are well formed in my heart. I will be a living sacrificial offering in Your Church. I am formed by You to be little, poor, hidden, silent, broken, and vulnerable. I do not protect myself from Love's Torrent. Because your greatest attribute is Mercy, I will be mercy for souls. I can do none of this but Your grace will make it a reality.

For what reason did You invade me? The reason is love. Your

Love is extravagant and must be poured out. I opened the door of my heart when You knocked. You have entered for good! I have never been more alive as when I undergo such diminishment! Knowing the cost of discipleship now, I choose You again. Forever, I choose You as my King and Lord.

Meditation and Prayer: With Mary on Calvary's Summit

Disciple

Lord Jesus, at the foot of the Cross you said, *"Behold your Mother."* I desire to ask our Holy Mother to grant understanding of the grace of Calvary, for there is no other who grasped the mystery of the Sacrifice and the heights of Divine Love present. Not only were you to give the greatest of gifts, your life for mine, but also, you gave your Holy Mother to me, to every person, in all ages. You know how great a need exists in the human heart for such a Mother uniquely united to the Most Holy Trinity. O Mother of the Redeemer, instruct me, please, in the way of love and sacrifice.

The Mother of the Redeemer

Disciple, how sorrowful was my heart at Calvary. My tears exhausted, my love began to be poured out too, as a libation upon Earth's children. As nestlings, I gathered my children to my Immaculate and Sorrowful Heart. As my heart was one with my Son's most Perfect Passion, here in my heart, I gather my children. Here in my heart, you find refuge. I am the Refuge of Sinners, *"Refugium Peccatorum."* See my love, my maternal guidance refashion your love for my Son, as of my love; a love that is pure, insatiable, tender, attentive, responsive, faithful, and above all these, sacrificial. A love that compels you and me to Calvary's Mount.

Disciple, can you imagine the horrific pain my heart endured to see my gentle Babe, He who is Innocence, to become as a Sin Offering. With each buffet, with each blasphemy, with each mockery, with each wound, with each curse and defilement, My Immaculate Heart was pierced by the noble sword of sorrow, compassion, and co-redemption. As my Son breathed His last breath, giving up the Spirit's breath, my final sword met its mark; my heart cleaved and pierced to become eternally one with that Sacred Heart of my Son.

Know this disciple: for every tear, every cry for mercy, every heart bruised and broken for the Passion of my Son, every heart that surrendered to the Redemption of His Blood along the Via Dolorosa, I gathered all of these precious gems of the merits of my Son's Redemption into my Most Immaculate Heart. On that terrible Good Friday, these merits gave me strength and comfort. Now this day as you join with my Son in His Passion, I gather these precious gems of merit into My Sorrowful Heart. As the Enemy was defeated at Calvary by the Crucifixion, so the Enemy is defeated in you by your own crucifixion. In your death to yourself, you are freed for the Love of my Son in the life of the Trinity!

Disciple, during this season of tremendous and precious grace let me gather you to Calvary. I do this for you in the Holy Mass in a special manner. Pray, too, the rosary. Pray my Son's Stations of the Cross. Meditate upon our Passion! Here is the wellspring of your love for our Hearts, Sacred and Immaculate.

Meditation: My God, My God, Why Has Thou Forsaken Me?

Disciple

My God, My God, why have Thou forsaken Me? Suddenly I am surrounded by darkness and my heart is deeply troubled. Do not hide Your Face from me, O God, for I am need of direction. In this valley of tears I find no consolation from my distress. My heart is cold and I feel alone in this world, cut off from love. I am losing hope and prayer seems futile. O God, in your mercy, hear my cry for help! My soul is sorrowful and searching for You. Open Your Heart and let a ray of Light pierce my darkness. Warm my heart by the fire of Divine Love. Be my strength, fortress and rock! Revive me from this deadness; bring me back to life. Show me the path to walk and grant peace to my soul

The Lord

Disciple, I cried out to the Eternal Father from my bed of wood when I was about to breathe My last before giving up My Spirit and expiring for love of you. I felt for that moment as you feel now, forgotten and alone, full of the pallor of death. I cried out to the heavens but was made to suffer this moment of separation from the tangible consolation of My Father, this Father whom I love infinitely. This is He who said: *"I will glorify You as You glorify Me."* For one brief moment then, silence was His reply and He permitted that I experience that abandonment of being separated from the grace of My own Father, of feeling forgotten by the Almighty One. This was yet another sacrifice of My humanity; that I would experience the agony of such a moment of disconnection and loneliness, of discouragement and sorrow.

Disciple, be patient and wait upon your God with hope in your heart. You know that you have been purchased by My Salvific Blood and that you belong not to yourself but to Me, to the family of the Most Holy Trinity. You are never alone! In the reality of the spiritual world, you are surrounded by the grace of the Sovereign Father, Son, and Holy Spirit.

In the moments of greatest distress when darkness overshadows your life, cling tightly to My Holy Cross and contemplating My Infinite and Merciful Love for you, remember that I died for your sins and opened the gates of heaven that you will enter My Courts with praise and thanksgiving as a child of the Most High, a disciple of the King of Kings and Lord of Lords. Would I have said that I was going to prepare a place for you if My plans were for your ruin?

Disciple, this fear and hopelessness that paralyzes your heart, constricts the flow of Divine Grace to cut off that Love present in your heart in the Person of the Holy Spirit. Truth is your pillar and foundation. Unite your suffering to Mine on the Cross, that time of complete surrender. If for a moment you receive only silence from God, know that the silence is pregnant with new life for you. Do as I did at Calvary; complete your mission, disciple! Complete it in faith and you will break through into new life. You are sustained by Grace and would cease to breathe if you were forgotten by God; for your Life's Breath is from Your Father. You live and move and have your being in the Perfect Charity of the family of the Father, Son, and Holy Spirit. Persevere, disciple!

✝

Meditation: Magdalene's Hymn of Praise and Prayer of Gratitude

Disciple

It is written, "accompanying Him were the Twelve and some women who had been cured of evil spirits, and infirmities, Mary, called Magdalene, from whom seven demons have gone out, Joanna, the wife of Herod's steward Chuza, Susanna, and many others who provided for them out of their resources." (Lk 8:2) From that moment when the Master healed your sin-sick soul, you followed and served the Lord from the onset of His ministry in Galilee to his death and beyond. The Lord healed your serious affliction, transformed you by the power of Divine Mercy. He bent down to pick you up from the ground and your heart was captured forever by the indescribable Beauty of Pure Love. The Lamb of God conquered your sin and led you to Life in Him. In gratitude you served Him, forever singing His praises, faithful in every circumstance, leading the lamentations along the Via Dolorosa and at the foot of the Cross, always by the side of the Virgin Mother of the Lamb. On the day of the Resurrection, you were the first witness of His Eternal Victory and told the apostle's the Truth. Mary of Magdala, pray for me to be converted from darkness into light.

Mary Magdalene Hymn of Praise

Rabbi, Teacher, Jesus, Savior, Messiah, and Lamb,
When I was lost in sin and did not recognize myself,
You did not condemn me to punishment or death.
Full of Perfect Charity, Your heart ablaze with Love,
Moved to pity for sinners, of whom I was the greatest,
You chose to forgive my transgressions freely.

Bending from the heights of Your Holiness,
You stooped to the ground to find me there
Wallowing in my sinful choices, seeking love

Without knowing what l was seeking after.
Driven by human passions, I walked with the spirits
Of darkness and shunned the light of Truth.

I saw myself fit for the darkness and tried to hide
Myself in the din of lustful and greedy desires.
This sinful heart became a whirlpool of contamination.
Driven by a lifestyle of disordered affection, I lost my way.
Shunned by the righteous and lawful people,
I became shame to those who beheld me and talked.

Then came that moment of Truth when our eyes met
For the first time and You knew everything about me.
You saw my blindness and sickness of soul.
You desired to heal and restore my soul to Order.
The balm of divine forgiveness broke over me;
My shame and scars were taken away.

You conquered your sinful servant
In the revelation of Your Divine Heart
Full of Mercy; you lavished your healing
Upon a heart mired in sin and darkness.
Your extravagant Love thoroughly cleansed,
And I was again born of Water and Spirit.

To be in Your service and the company of Miriam,
To care for the needs of apostles and holy women,
Was the honor given unto me and the fruit of contrition?
The fire of Divine Charity set ablaze my heart,
When You took my hand in Your Own and
Revealed, "I Am the Way, the Truth, and the Life."

I witnessed your passion, death and resurrection;
I saw the terrible price you paid for my sins,
The river of tears that flooded the face of Our Mother
At the foot of that Cross of Salvation on Calvary's Hill.
Through countless days of ages and then some

I sing my hymn of gratitude and praise of Your Mercy.

The Choirs of Angels proclaim Your Majesty.
The Apostles, Prophets, and Saints above and below
Give endless thanksgiving and honor to You, Lord.
Your wounds forever heal the sins of creation,
Sinners are found covered in Your Precious Blood.
Hosanna to the King and glory to Him forever!

✝
Meditation:
The Fourth Word of Jesus on the Cross

Quote: **Anne Catherine Emmerich**

Stillness reigned around the Cross. Jesus hung upon it alone; forsaken by all, disciples, followers, friends, his Mother even removed from His side; not one person of the thousands upon whom He had lavished benefits was near to offer Him the slightest alleviation in his bitter agony, his Soul overspread with an indescribable feeling of bitterness and grief, all within Him was dark and gloomy and wretched. The darkness which reigned around was but symbolic of that which overspread his interior; he turned, nevertheless, to His Heavenly Father. He prayed for his enemies, He offered the chalice of his sufferings for the redemption, He continued to pray as He had done during the whole of his Passion, and repeated portions of the Psalms the prophecies of which were then receiving their accomplishment in Him.

I saw angels standing around. Again I looked at Jesus, my Beloved Spouse, on his Cross, agonizing and dying, yet still in dreary solitude. He at that moment endured anguish which no mortal pen can describe, he felt that suffering which would overwhelm a poor weak mortal if deprived at once of all consolation, both divine and human, and then compelled, without refreshment, assistance, or light, to traverse the stormy desert of tribulation, upheld by faith, hope, and charity alone.

His sufferings were inexpressible; but it was by them that he merited for us the grace necessary to resist those temptations to despair which will assail us at the hour of death, that tremendous hour when we shall feel that we are about to leave all that is dear to us here below. When our minds, weakened by disease, have lost the power of reasoning, and even our hopes of mercy and forgiveness are become, as it were, enveloped in mist and uncertainty, that it is that we must fly to Jesus, unite our feelings of desolation with that indescribable dereliction, which he endured upon the Cross, and be certain of obtaining a glorious victory over our infernal enemies. Jesus then offered to his Eternal Father his poverty, his dereliction, his labors, and, above all, the bitter sufferings which our ingratitude had caused Him to endure in expiation for our sins and weaknesses; no one, therefore, who is united to Jesus in the bosom of his Church must despair at the awful moment preceding his exit from this life, even if he be deprived of all sensible light and comfort, for He must then remember that the Christian is no longer obliged to enter this dark desert alone and unprotected, as Jesus has cast his own interior and exterior dereliction on the Cross into this gulf of desolation; consequently He will not be left to cope alone with death, or be suffered to leave this world in desolation of spirit, deprived of heavenly consolation. All fear of loneliness and despair in death must therefore be cast away; for Jesus, who is our true light, *the Way, the Truth, and the Life*, has preceded us on that dreary road, has overspread it with blessings, and raised His Cross upon it, one glance at which will calm our every fear.

Jesus then (if we may so express ourselves) made His last testament in the presence of his Father, and bequeathed the merits of his Death and Passion to the Church and to sinners. Not one erring soul was forgotten; he thought of each and every one; praying, likewise, even for those heretics who have endeavored to prove that, being God, He did not suffer as a man would have suffered in his place. The cry which he allowed to pass his lips in the height of his agony was intended not only to show the excess of the sufferings He was enduring, but likewise to encourage all afflicted souls who acknowledge God as their Father to lay their sorrows with filial confidence at his feet. It was towards three o'clock when he cried out in a loud voice, *"Eloi, Eloi, lamma sabacthani?"* *"My God, my God, why hast Thou forsaken Me?"* These words of Our Lord interrupted the silence which had continued for so long the Pharisees turned towards Him, and one of them said, *"Behold, he calleth Elias"* and another *"Let us see whether Elias will come to deliver him."* When Mary heard the voice of her Divine Son, she was unable to restrain herself any longer, but rushed forwards to the foot of the Cross, followed by John, Mary, the daughter of Cleophas, Mary Magdalen, and Salome.

Quote: *The Dolorous Passion of Our Lord Jesus Christ*
Anne Catherine Emmerich, Tan Publishers, 1968, pgs. 287, 288

Prayer: The Scriptural Way of The Cross

1. Jesus Is Condemned To Death

God so loved the world that He gave His only-begotten Son to save it. (John 3:16)

Though He was harshly treated, He submitted and opened not His mouth; like a lamb led to the slaughter or a sheep before the shearers, He was silent and opened not his mouth. (Is. 53:7)

Greater love than this no one has, that one lay down his life for his friends. (John 15:13)

2. Jesus Bears His Cross

It was our infirmities that He bore, our sufferings that He endured. (Is.53:4)

If anyone wishes to come after Me, let him deny himself, and take up his cross daily, and follow Me. (Luke 9:23)

Take My yoke upon you and learn from me. For My yoke is easy and My burden light. (Matt. 11:28-29)

3. Jesus Falls the First Time

He has broken My teeth with gravel, pressed My Face in the dust; My soul is deprived of peace, I have forgotten what happiness is. (Lam. 3:16-17)

The Lord laid upon Him the guilt of us all. (Is. 53:6)

Behold, the Lamb of God, Who takes away the sin of the world! (John 1:29)

4. Jesus Meets His Mother

Did you not know that I must be about My Father's business? (Luke 2:49)

Come, all you who pass by the way, look and see whether there is any suffering like My suffering. (Lam. 1:12).

You have sorrow now; but I will see you again, and your heart shall rejoice, and your joy no one shall take from you. (John 16:22)

5. Jesus is Helped By Simon

As long as you did it for one of these, the least of my brethren, you did it for Me. (Matt.25:40)

Bear one another's burdens, and so you will fulfill the law of Christ. (Gal. 6:2)

No servant is greater than his master. (John 13:16)

6. Veronica Wipes the Face of Jesus

His look was marred beyond that of man, and His appearance beyond that of mortals. (Is. 52:14)

He who sees Me, sees also the Father. (John 14:9)

The Son is the brightness of the Father's glory and the image of His substance. (Heb. 1:3)

7. Jesus Falls a Second Time

I was hard pressed and was falling, but the Lord helped me. (Ps. 118, 13)

We have not a high priest who cannot have compassion on our infirmities, but One tried as we are in all things except sin. (Heb. 4:15)

Come to Me, all you who labor and are burdened, and I will give you rest. (Matt. 11:28)

8. Jesus Speaks to the Women

Daughters of Jerusalem, do not weep for Me, but weep for yourselves and for your children. (Luke 23:28)

If anyone does not abide in Me, he shall be cast outside as the branch and wither. (John 15:6)

Unless you repent, you will all perish. (Luke 13:3)

9. Jesus Falls a Third Time

I am like water poured out; all my bones are racked, My heart had become like wax. My throat is dried up like baked clay; My tongue cleaves to My jaws; to the dust of death you have brought Me down. (Ps.22, 15-16)

Have this mind in you which was also in Jesus Who emptied Himself, taking the nature of a slave. (Phil. 2:5-7).

Everyone who exalts himself shall be humbled, and he who humbles himself shall be exalted. (Luke 14:11)

10. Jesus Is Stripped Of His Garments

They divide my garments among them, and for My vesture they cast lots. (Ps. 22, 19)

Every one of you who does not renounce all that he possesses can not be My Disciple. (Luke 14:33)

Put on the Lord Jesus Christ, and as for the flesh, take no thought for its lust. (Rom. 13:14).

11. Jesus Is Nailed To The Cross

They have pierced My hands and My feet; I can count all My bones. (Ps. 22, 17-18).

Father, forgive them for they do not know what they are doing. (Luke 23:34)

I have come down from heaven, not to do My will, but the will of Him Who sent Me. (John 6:38)

12. Jesus Dies On The Cross

And I, if I be lifted up from the earth, will draw all things to Myself. (John 12:32)

Father, into your hands I commend My spirit. (Luke 23:46)

He humbled Himself, becoming obedient to death, even to death on a cross. Therefore God also has exalted Him. (Phil. 2:8-9)

13. Jesus is Taken Down from the Cross

Did not the Christ have to suffer those things before entering into His glory? (Luke 24:26)

Those who love Your law have great peace. (Ps. 119, 165)

In this has the love of God been shown in our case that God has sent His only-begotten Son into the world as a propitiation from sins. (John 4:9-10)

14. Jesus Is Placed in the Tomb

Unless the grain of wheat falls into the ground and dies, it remains alone. But if it dies, it brings forth much fruit. (John 12:24-25)

The death that Christ died, He died to sin once for all, but the life the He lives, He lives unto God. Thus do you consider your selves also as dead to sin, but alive to God in Christ Jesus. (Rom. 6:10-11)

Christ rose again the third day, according to the Scriptures. (1 Cor. 15, 3-4)

Meditation and Prayer: "I Thirst"

The Lord

Disciple, I make all things new! I have taken the white rose of your heart and I have colored it with My Passion. Let your heart become crimson, disciple. Let your pure heart blush with the passion of My suffering and death. Disciple, trust in My Loving plan for you. I receive your family into the Eternal Wellspring of My Most Sacred Heart. Is there not room here for them? Do I not keep My promises? Disciple, by your intercession I have gathered your family into My Heart. I ask you to release them fully into My embrace. Your love will not be lessened for them rather it will only be strengthened and purified. Together, in My Heart, we can do much for your family.

Disciple, I call you to keenly experience My Passion this Lent. As a Bridegroom calls out to His beloved, I cry out to you in My thirst, in My loneliness, and My weariness upon the wood of the Cross. Will you comfort Me, My beloved? Will you brush My bloody hair from My eyes, so that I might look upon you, My beloved? Let us speak softly to one another words of sweet comfort and fidelity. Let your tears, your weeping become the song of our love.

Disciple

Lord, I desire to sing the song of our love and to please You in all things. Your love demands a complete surrender and I desire to give this to You. I believe that You make all things new and await Your promises. Augment my faith in You. See how I need to grow in my faith and trust! Help me, Lord Jesus to abandon myself and my family unto your Merciful Heart. You Passion blushes in my heart and I feel the rush your Precious Blood washing over my heart, my will, my mind, my life. Transform me into a white rose of purity and let my heart become crimson with the red blood of your Passion.

The Lord

Disciple, I strengthen you for the holy tasks at hand. Gather my people to the Mantle of Our Mother. Here at Calvary, let My Blood sprinkle upon the hearts of My children. Let them be anointed in My Passion. Learn from the Blessed of Mothers.

Disciple, I sing to you this hour of My sweet solicitude for My bride. Gather at My feet like Magdalene and let your tears perfume My feet. Did I not raise up Magdalene to become My apostle of Love? Be strengthened in My Love. Know that I am with you always. The Passion of My Heart will never cease.

Disciple

Lord Jesus, Redeemer of my soul and Savior of mankind, I desire to satisfy your Divine Thirst. Grant that I may give unto You the purest love of my heart. I love You with a love that is small and imperfect. I ask now for the grace to have your Sacred Heart for my own. Jesus, I desire to exchange my little heart for your Sacred Heart that I may satisfy your perpetual thirst. All that I have is from You. There is nothing I can give back to You that isn't given to me from Your Heart. Trusting that you desire for me to quench your thirst I ask that I may do so from the wellspring of Your Own Heart and therefore enlarge my offering to You. I release my family and intentions into Your Heart of Infinite, Perfect Charity. Satisfy my thirst for love O Lord, that I may satisfy Your Divine Thirst. Until all love is consummated at the end of the ages when there will be no more thirst, let us give one another to drink of the streams of our love.

Meditation:
Behold the Man: the Pope Crucified

Jesus, in the person of John Paul II,
Is the mirror of Your Crucified image.
This Holy Pontiff radiates pure love.
Bent from the weight upon his shoulders,
He carries the Cross as his standard.
He raises The Wood high for all to see.
A signpost of Truth travels the world.
In the present darkness of this age,
He shines like a beacon of heavenly light.

Lord, You give a saint to lead the Church.
A man of sanctity teaches the Way.
He pours himself out like a libation.
Daily he is your Ambassador of Love.
He never ceases to amaze the nations
With supernatural wisdom and
Zeal for Your holy House.
He points the way to the future of springtime.

Holding tightly to the Cross he leans on,
A prophet for this generation speaking,
A visionary for ages to come writing history,
Laying the foundation of hope for the future,
He proclaims an ideal based on the Gospel.
He is a living gospel written in Blood.
He proclaims glad tidings to the poor.
In His Face we see Your Goodness.
Holiness adorns him and we are attracted.
He beckons the Church to conversion.

The human family is his family
Each person full of human dignity,

A child of the Most High God,
None are forgotten in his heart
He looks to the youth to carry on
The treasury of the faith;
The gospel of life and
The Eucharistic Sacrifice.

O Lord, extend his life for our sake,
Strengthen his body for the mission.
His spirit continues, strong as ever.
You uphold him in the palm of Your Hand.
O God, You are Sovereign and
With You all things are possible.
Grant this "Totus Tuus" Pontiff
Extended length of days and
Protect him from all harm, and bless him
For the completion of his holy mission.

Consecration to the Mother of the Sacrifice

Mother Mary

Disciple, love is always a sacrifice. If you really love one another properly, there must be a sacrifice. My Son showed you by example, the way of love is the Way of the Cross. Do not let your heart be troubled when you feel the weight of the Cross bearing down upon your life. Like a woman who suffers pangs of birth to bring forth her child, suffering wrapped in Love can bring forth an abundance of new life for you.

At the foot of the Cross, My Savior Son gave the command, "Woman, Behold your son." In that time and place, the Redeemer of the world set in motion my Universal Motherhood ordaining that I would take all people and nations into the realm of My Immaculate Heart to nourish them with spiritual food. He set me to be their Advocate before the Throne of the Trinity, to be their Co-Redemptrix, gaining grace through the Perfect Sacrifice of the Lamb. Because our Two Hearts are as one Heart of Love, we were pierced in unity of the Spirit. His Adorable and Sacred Heart was pierced physically and mystically. My Maternal Heart was pierced by the sword of sorrow with a mystical thrust that would have caused me to expire if I had not been given the Grace needed to sustain such a blow! My Heart was broken open with His for you and for all generations to come. He has willed this to be a grace for you and the world.

Disciple

O Mother of heaven and earth, my Queen, I need only to look inside your Immaculate Heart to find the virtues of sanctity and the radiance of pure love unique to the Mother of God. I desire to consecrate my heart and life, all that I am and all that I have, to your maternal solicitude and give you permission to use whatever merits I may have before God for the intentions of Your Immaculate Heart. You know how best to make use of my little offerings. I trust that you will impart the graces best suited for my soul and the mission that God has given to me. Your heart is the world's treasury of grace and for me it is a wellspring of wisdom, protection, and love. Mother, teach me to pray from the heart and to grow wise by God's standard. Make use of my consecration and allow me to work for through Your Maternal Heart for the glory of God and salvation of souls.

O Mother, you have always been the chosen fountain of grace for the world. Your fiat made possible the Incarnation. In your chosen womb The Word became Flesh. How glorious were those years in Nazareth when you enjoyed the love of St. Joseph and Jesus in the privacy of your hidden life. From your humble home arose a column of incense, the prayers and love of the holy family rising to the Father in heaven and making intercession for the world. But you did not hold too tightly to Your Son, for you knew the purpose of His Life on earth was to suffer and die and rise again. Mother, I pray that our family will become holy and our house a sanctuary of selfless love. We are in need of your maternal protection and guidance. Allow me to offer intercession through your Immaculate Heart.

Mother Mary

Disciple, by means of your Act of Consecration, I am free to unite maternal grace to your offering and magnify the fruit of your intercession and sacrifice. Through your consecration to my heart, you more easily and more swiftly arrive in the depths of the Sacred Heart of My Son. God so honors the freedom of the human will that He requires your cooperation with Divine Grace and awaits your permission to use you to build up the Mystical Body of Christ. When you consecrate your heart to mine, you allow me to help you more, you free my maternal hand to reach out for you. I gather all of God's children into my maternal love but those who are consecrated to my Heart form an army of souls bound together by the desire to be useful for my works of Grace for souls, the Church and world. Do you see now why your consecration is a grace and gift to both of us?

Disciple

Mother, I place myself in the refuge of your heart and pray that I may live out my consecration with generosity of heart and humility of spirit. I claim nothing for myself but give all to you to distribute for the honor and glory of God. Humble Spouse of the Holy Spirit, let His Breath permeate my being and give new life to my prayers and sacrifices. Only in the power of the Holy Spirit am I able to fully live my consecration. With you by my side, with the Holy Spirit as my breath, I am not afraid to walk the Via Dolorosa and become a mirror of Christ Crucified. Seat of Wisdom, instruct your disciple that I may live in the light of the Truth. Amen.

Overcoming Evil by the Power of the Cross

The Lord

Disciple, I know that your journey is wrought with danger from the Evil One who proudly professed that he will not serve God and vowed to make war upon the offspring of the "Woman Crowned with Twelve Stars." Do you see whose heel is positioned over his serpent head to crush him at will? Disciple, do you understand now that your Mother is a warrior too, full of the grace to offer protection for you?

The Evil One tempts you to put down your cross and run away from it, seeking relief from suffering. He is incapable of love and knows nothing of its sacrifice but you are created for love, and this requires sacrifice. It is written that his name is "Liar, the father of all lies" and this is how he entraps you with lies of liberation from all suffering, lies of happiness in selfish and sinful pursuits. He tempted Me at Calvary and asked Me to get down from the Cross when he realized that I had overcome eternal death and opened heaven for all ages.

Disciple

Lord, help me to put on the armor that you provide for me. I desire to fight against all that is unholy in me and to change my environment into something holy. Lord, stand guard at the doorway of my house and grant angelic protection from the evil that assails my soul and my household. The more fervor I have for You and Your House, the more I deny myself and take up my cross, the more the enemy pursues and attacks from every direction. Grant that I may know the difference between my spirit, Your Holy Spirit and the Evil Spirit. Grant that I do not open the door to the evil one through the faults of my own Capital Sins. If I know my weakness and humble myself before You, Lord, grant that I may quickly banish the evil that surrounds me.

The Lord

Satan tempts you to get off of the Cross and go your own way of false security. He tempts you to walk the journey alone so you are easy prey for him and his legions. Disciple, you never walk the royal road of the cross alone. Your brothers and sisters are there to be your Simon of Cyrene and I repeat the pattern of My Footsteps for you, taking most of the weight of your cross upon My Shoulder again. I have shown you the way of sacrificial love and provided a fountain of grace through Holy Mother Church. Lean on My Mystical Body, My Priesthood and Sacraments and you will have all that you need to wrap your arms around the cross in your life and experience the joy of discipleship. The power of the Holy Spirit will produce good fruit through your sacrifice. You honor My solemn Good Friday Sacrifice to prepare for the gift of the Resurrection. The Tomb is empty. I have already come forth and you, too, shall rise again with Me!

Disciple, do not be afraid. Do you not understand the devil is afraid of you? The more you become My Image, the more he fears you. The power within you is greater than any power of his. For I have poured the grace of the Holy Spirit into your heart to make you a fortified city of courageous love. Humility, obedience, and love drive the Enemy away. Two by two I sent my early disciples. Two by two I send you. Two fortify one another and keep the heart ablaze with the Love that casts out fear. Disciple, hold fast to the cross and live by its standard, and your enemy will flee. Fear not!

Meditation and Prayer: By His Wounds You Have Been Healed (1 Peter 2:24)

It is written: "When He was insulted, He returned no insult; when He suffered, He did not threaten; instead, He handed himself over to the one who judges justly. He himself bore our sins in His Body upon the Cross, so that free from sin, we might live for righteousness. By His Wounds you have been healed. For you had gone astray like sheep, but you have now returned to the Shepherd and Guardian of your souls." (1 Peter 2:24)

Disciple

O Lord, my Savior, grant me the grace to be healed by Your Holy Wounds. You see clearly the wounds I bear in my heart and body: hurts from the past that still press upon my daily journey, the memories of injuries of long ago, and injustices done unto me that leave a scar in my heart. You see the marks of my own sins too, staining my soul and eroding true life from my spirit.

O Lord, grant that I may become free to love, healed from all that enslaves my heart, and ties me to base things so I do not soar in the Spirit, and not free to rise to the holiness of life that You must desire for me. Grant that I may be purified in the living waters of your Spirit, washed completely clean in the Blood that flows from Your Pierced Heart.

The Lord

Disciple, the desires of your heart are known to Me. Your prayer is born of the Holy Spirit who prays within you. More than you seek to be healed, I desire to bring you into wellness of body, mind, and spirit. The wounds of past injustices, the deprivations you have experienced, and the unloving actions of others towards you, should be placed into My Holy Wounds for I have already delivered you from these on that day of the One True Sacrifice that suffices for all eternity. I have already healed you when you choose to forgive the unloving actions of others, when you follow My example of

Mercy from the Cross. There, I did not profess the guilt of every person in the family of man but begged the Father's forgiveness upon you. Forgiveness of each person who wounded you, forgiveness of yourself, too, forgiveness of God; these are keys to healing the wounds of body, mind and spirit. If you desire these keys, the grace is given from heaven. You must then use these keys to unlock the iron walls you placed around your heart to protect yourself and become vulnerable to love again.

The wounds of your own sinfulness, the choices you made in error, the scars from your own failure to love and serve others, the injuries you have brought onto yourself through choosing the way of the world, all of these, should be taken in haste to the Sacrament of My Mercy. The Confessional is where I await you and believe that it is I in that priestly chair! Come to Me there and the floodgates of Mercy will wash over your sin-sick soul, and I shall dispense Divine Mercy through My priest son. You shall be free then to begin again on the straight and narrow path, unencumbered and full of grace from heaven. You know you are well again when your heart is not hardened but vulnerable, when My peace that surpasses all understanding is present in your heart. A sure sign of being healed is when your joy in Me becomes strong and praise rises up in your heart. Humility, that is truth, is present in the soul that is healed, and from this comes the grace to love in a sacrificial manner. When you are engaged in the art of loving others before yourself, you mirror My example and live My teaching. Become a living Gospel! Believe in your healing!

When you approach the altar of Sacrifice in My Church, come humbly before Me and pray from the heart the words repeated at each Holy Mass, *"Lord, I am not worthy to receive you but only say the word and I shall be healed."* My Body and Blood are your daily medicine. Do not deprive yourself of this Divine Medicine that heals all wounds in and through the Sacrifice. Disciple, I am the Medicine for your wounds and Healer is My Name. Come to My Mercy and receive your healing.

Meditation: For Good Friday

Quote: **St. Gertrude the Great**

As the passion was read, at the word *"Sitio"* (I Thirst), Our Lord appeared to offer her a golden cup to receive the tears of compassion which she had shed for His death. And as the Saint felt her whole soul melting into tears, and yet discretion obliged her to keep them back, she asked Our Lord what would be most pleasing to Him. Then it appears to her that a pure rivulet sprang from her heart, and proceeded to Our Lord's lips, and He said: *"These are the tears of devotion which you have restrained from a pure intention"*.

At Terce, as she remembered Our Lord's crowning with thorns, His cruel scourging at the pillar, His weariness, and the agony of His shoulder, wounded by carrying the Cross, she said to Him, *"Behold, my sweetest Lord, I offer Thee my heart desiring to suffer therein all the bitterness and anguish of Thy dear Heart, in return for Thy Love in bearing the undeserved torments of Thy Passion; and I beseech Thee, whenever I forget this offering through human frailty to send me some sharp bodily pain which may resemble Thine."* He replied: *"Your desires are sufficient. But is you wish Me to have unbounded pleasure in your heart, let Me act as I please therein, and do not desire that I should give you either consolation or suffering."*

When the Passion was read that says that Joseph took the Body of Jesus, she said to Our Lord: *"That blessed Joseph was given Thy most Holy Body; but what share wilt Thou give of Thy Body to my unworthiness?"* Then Our Lord gave her His Heart under the form of a golden thurible, from which as many perfumes ascended to the Father as there had been persons for whom the Lord died.

When the prayers were said after the Passion for the different Orders in the Church, according to the usual custom, as the priest knelt, say *Oremus, delectissimi,* she saw all the prayers which had been made throughout the Church ascending together like fragrant incense from the thurible of the Divine Heart, so that each prayer by this union became marvelously sweet and beautiful.

Therefore, we should pray for the Church on this day with great devotion, in union with the Passion of Our Lord, which renders our prayers more efficacious before God."

…The Saint, ardently desiring to make some return to her Beloved for all His sufferings, said to Him: *"O my only Hope, and Salvation of my soul! Teach me how to make some return to Thee for Thy most bitter Passion."*

Our Lord replied, *"He who follows the will of another, and not his own frees Me from the captivity which I endured when bound with chains on the morning of My Passion; he who considers himself guilty, satisfies for my condemnation, at the hour of Prime, by false witnesses; he who renounces the pleasures of sense, consoles Me for the blows which I received at the hour of Terce; he who submits to pastors who try him, consoles me for the crowning of thorns; he who humbles himself first in a dispute, carries My Cross; he who performs works of charity, consoles Me at the hour of Sext, when My limbs were cruelly fastened to the Cross; he who spares himself neither pain nor labor to withdraw his neighbor from sin, consoles Me for My Death, which I endured at the hour of None for the salvation of the human race; he who replies gently when reproached, takes Me down from the Cross; lastly, he who prefers his neighbor to himself, lays Me in the sepulcher."*

On another Good Friday, as Gertrude sought Our Lord to prepare her for a worthy Communion, she received this reply: *"I am hastening to you with such ardor that I can scarcely contain it; for I have gathered into My bosom all the good which My Church has done or said or thought today in memory of My Passion, to pour it forth into your soul at Communion for your eternal salvation."* The Saint replied: *"I give Thee thanks, O my Lord; but I desire greatly that this favor may be granted to me in such a manner that I may impart it to others when I wish to do so."* He replied: *"And what will you give Me, my beloved, for such a favor?"* Gertrude replied: *"Alas, Lord! I have nothing worthy of Thee; but nevertheless, I have this desire, that if I had all that Thou hast, I would give it to Thee, so that Thou might dispose of it as Thou would desire."* To this Our Lord replied lovingly: *"If you do indeed desire to act thus toward Me, you cannot doubt that I desire to act thus toward you; and even more so, since My goodness and love so far exceed yours."* *"O God, how shall I come to Thee, when Thou come to me with such abundant goodness?"* He replied: *"I require nothing from you but to come to Me empty, that I may fill you; for it is from Me that you receive all which makes you agreeable in My sight."*

Quote: *The Life and Revelations of St. Gertrude the Great* By **St. Gertrude**, Tan Publishers, 2002 edition, pages 374, 375, 376.

Prayer of Praise:
Roses of Honor for Five Holy Wounds

Disciple

O Jesus, I desire to run to You at the foot of the Cross with arms full of roses to lay at your Holy Cross in honor of Your Five Precious Wounds. May these roses represent the gift of my heart, the sacrifices I want to make for the glory of Your Holy Name? I do not know how to sing your praises like the angels and saints and psalmist who have done so in magnificent hymns of praise, poems of love. But I do know how to gather roses from my heart's garden as a little sign of my deep affection and gratitude for Your Holy Wounds. As I run to Your Cross, with my arms full of these little offerings, I want to gaze in silence at My Savior veiled in death's disguise. Moved by Your Sacrifice of Love, I wish to place my offerings inside each Wound.

In the Wound of Your Right Hand, I place the rose of my human will. I rest it in that Wound of Yours so my human will does not become my wound too. Grant that I may exchange it for the Divine Will in my life. In Your Right Hand, my human will shall become a sweet fragrance; an offering I make from the depths of my heart in appreciation for Your Death on the Cross.

In the Wound of Your Left Hand, I place the rose of my human senses, consecrating them to You so they become attuned to what is Holy and desire only the good things of God, not the futile things of the world. Purify my senses in the Wound of Your Left Hand and make holy these faculties given to me for Your Glory and Honor.

In the Wound of Your Feet, I place the roses of my loved ones, my family that mean so much to me. They will be safer there in the Wound of Your Holy Feet because you walked the Way of the Cross for them and Divine Love is far above the way of my human love. My family bows down before You, O Savior. You humbled Yourself and became wounded for us. Now we humble ourselves in the Wounds of Your Holy Feet.

In the Wound of Your Sacred Head, crowned with terrible thorns, I place the roses of my past, present, and future. I give these to You as a sign of fidelity to Your Law of Love and an affirmation of my trust in Divine Providence. Those "Thorns of Torture" represented my sins of past, present, and future. Now I surrender unto You these roses to perfume and anoint your Holy Head Wounds. Grant that I lean not on human understanding of my past, present and future but surrender them completely to You. My Crucified King crowned by mockery, may I remove the thorns and place roses?

In the Wound of Your Pierced Side and Heart, I place the rose of my heart as a sign that I desire to be Yours completely. Grant that I no longer exist outside of Your Sacred Heart. Divine Charity compelled You to desire Baptism by Fire and die for my sins. Your Pierced Heart is truly a King's Castle and I long to live there. In the spilling of Your Precious Blood, I was washed clean and am able now to put on white gowns of purity. I am able now to approach Your Gates and enter with praise and thanksgiving. O Jesus, I adore You and will sing forever my hymn of praise and gratitude. Mercy is mine! Thank You, My Savior. All the days of my life may I lay roses at your Feet and honor your Holy Wounds. May this be a "Covenant of Love" that is pleasing to You. Grant that my life form beautiful roses of sacrifice for You. On Calvary's Hill may they bloom. Amen.

Meditation: Through the Holy Spirit, He Offered Himself

Quote: **Most Rev. Luis Martinez**

God wills many things that are in reality but one thing. For unity is the mark of all that is His, a rich unity that holds the universe in magnificent harmony. The human artist, in his masterpiece, wills and arranges all the elements, the lights and shadows, colors and figures, seeking in this variety a central theme that will unify and harmonize the artistic elements, and which is the key to the world and the reason for its beauty.

The Divine Artist has willed many things: the earth with all its marvels, history and all its vicissitudes, the supernatural order with all its prodigies. Yet among this immense variety, His gaze, His search, His love, are only for Jesus Crucified.

The Cross is the key to God's magnificent work, the secret of its unity and beauty, the coordinating principle of the world and history, of time and eternity. Therefore, St. Paul could say that the Will of the Father was accomplished by the oblation of the Body of Christ, and that we are sanctified in that Will.

The devotion to the Father that filled the soul of Jesus, that soul great beyond measure, had the Cross for its terminus. Only on the Cross was His longing to glorify the Father satisfied, His immense hunger for doing the Will of the Father appeased; on there did His infinite Love attain rest.

The loving dream of Jesus during His mortal life was the Cross; He longed for it as only the heart of the Man-God could long for the culmination of all His infinite aspirations. Although He hid His supreme secret under the mantle of divine serenity, it escaped Him as a perfume escapes its containing vial. It undoubtedly revealed itself at Nazareth, to be received in Mary's heart, and again, in intimate conversations with His Apostles, as when He said, *"I have a baptism to be baptized with; and how distressed I am until it is accomplished,"* and that other time in the Cenacle, when He told His disciples of His ardent desire to celebrate the Pasch with them.

Jesus carried in His heart for thirty-three years the cruel, torturing martyrdom of longing for sacrifice, and of waiting for the hour appointed by the heavenly Father. Therefore, His devotion to the Father had a definitive form—sacrifice; a clear symbol—the Cross, and a precise formula—"Christ…through the Holy Spirit offered Himself unblemished unto God."

The Sanctifier by **Most Rev. Luis Martinez**, pages. 103, 104 Pauline Books and Media, Boston, 1995 edition.

Prayer: Holy Spirit Help Me to Drink the Chalice

Come Holy Spirit! Come Sanctifier! Overshadow my soul! Pierce my heart with your sword of Truth. Fire of Divine Love, purify my heart and life. Sanctify your temple and fill me with your wisdom to know myself so I may know My Lord and follow him all the way to Calvary's Summit of Love. Consecrate me in the truth of my salvation and never let me be led astray by the spirit of the world. Grant that I may be wise in discerning the spirits that surround my soul.

Strengthen my heart for baptism by fire. Fortify my soul to drink fully the chalice that is offered to me. In the power of Your Transforming Love, may I walk the way of the Cross daily and learn from The Master who set the path before me. May I discover the infinite treasures that are yet hidden in the Divine Plan for my journey through the embrace of the Cross. Through perpetual surrender, may I become sanctified and make reparation for sins. Grant that I am not crushed by the weight of the Cross but uplifted by the promise of its grace and fruit.

Holy Spirit, point out for me the Simon of Cyrene who will help me along the way. Humble me to accept the offer of the help that I need to carry my cross with love and joy. The Redeemer Himself needed the assistance of Simon of Cyrene. Who am I to think that I can carry my cross without human assistance?

Holy Spirit, prepare my heart to receive the Majestic Truth of Divine Love revealed in the person of Christ Crucified. Make useful my little sacrifices of love. Bless me with the charisms that I need to fulfill the unique mission of my soul in the Church. Imprint the Image of the Savior upon my life and allow me to become a reflection of His Perfect Charity.

Holy Spirit, offer your praises through me and teach me the way of prayer and sacrifice. Amen.

Meditation: Mass and Communion are Inseparable from Calvary

Quote: On the Teachings of **St. Therese of Lisieux**
You must realize throughout your life, at each step, you will find the Cross of your Divine Model, your King, crucified and crowned with thorns, Jesus. Humiliation is a bitter cross. Abandonment is a real crucifixion when it is rightly understood.

Mass and Communion are inseparable from Calvary. There is no reparation without penance and sacrifice. In the apostolate, the money to buy souls is suffering, accepted with love. Suppress the cross in your life, and everything crumbles. The cross is the structure. As it bore the Savior, it bears salvation, and so it must bear us also, and all our works.

Never look at the Cross without Jesus. If I must bear the cross all alone, I renounce it in advance. I do not want to touch the onerous burden with the end of my finger; I am too weak, too cowardly, and too sensitive. It is too hard to suffer. I deserve a hundred times to suffer without You, Jesus, but it is with You that I want to suffer. With You, I accept all the crosses, all of them, if you will bear them with me. You can hide Yourself, You can make it look as though You are not there, as if I am bearing it all alone, I accept that on one condition: that You hide yourself in my heart.

How can we be Christians, the subjects of a King crowned with thorns, baptized in his Blood, absolved so often by His Blood, receiving Communion every day at Mass, at his Sacrifice, and yet run away from the cross? That would be to forget that the cross is a marvelous invention of divine mercy that gives us the occasion to prove to Jesus that we love him. What is a love that does not prove itself? I told you that love is a choice. What merit is there in choosing Jesus if only we have to follow him on a path of roses? How would we know whether it was He or the roses on the pathway which we were following? He wants to be loved for himself, not for his gifts. He does not want the experience of the rich who lose their friends when they lose their money and can no longer give presents.

He is jealous of our true love. Without the Cross there would be many more faithful in the world; but would these be loving souls? For all eternity he wants to be able to thank us for having chosen Him, in sacrifice, for having shared His Cross with Him. When He gives us something to suffer, said little Therese, it is because He wants a gift from us. What gift? "A smile on the Cross." He begs for our love, proven by suffering, in order to be able to say, "It is you who remained with me in the trial." How sweet it will be when we head, for all eternity, these words from the lips of Jesus, or rather from the depths of His Heart: "And you are they who have continued with me in my temptations; and I dispose to You, as my Father has disposed to me, a kingdom, that you may eat and drink at my table, in My kingdom." (Lk 22:28)

Quote: *I Believe In Love* by **Pere Jean du Coeur de Jesus D'Elbee**, St. Bede's Publications, Petersham, Massachusetts, pages.119, 120.

Prayer to Unite My Holy Communion with His Sacrifice

O Lord, when I approach Your Altar of Sacrifice at Mass, when You humble yourself to come into my soul, may I humble myself before You and recall at the moment, the price You paid, every drop of Your Blood. When Your Body, Blood, Soul and Divinity, saturates my soul with Divine Mercy, may I respond in gratitude of Calvary and remembrance of Good Friday. I was baptized into Your death that I may have eternal life. Impress upon my heart the perpetual memory of Your Sacrifice so the infinite merits of Your Pierced Heart become a steady stream of Grace. May Your Sacrifice ignite a fire that never ceases to burn in my heart and fill me with praise and gratitude. O Sacrament of Love, at every Mass I pray that I am healed. At Holy Communion I give thanks that it is by Your Stripes that I am healed. When I receive the Cup may I remember that You drank it first for love of Me and never fail to respond in utmost generosity. With every Holy Communion may I unite to Your Sacrifice and live it. Amen.

Meditation: The Divine Lover's Farewell

Quote: **Fulton J. Sheen**

When Our Lord was baptized in the Jordan, the Holy Spirit came upon Him. He was baptized in the Spirit; but He must suffer before giving that Spirit to others. That is why, the night when His Passion began, He spoke most profoundly of the Spirit. In His conversation with the woman at the well, He said the time was come when true worshippers would worship: "God is spirit, and those who worship him must worship in spirit and in truth." (Jn.4:23)

His words "in Spirit" did not mean a contrast between an internal or sentimental religion as contrasted with external observances, but rather a contrast between a worship inspired by the Spirit of God as opposed to a purely natural spirit. "In Truth" did not mean "sincere and honest, " but rather I Christ, who is the Word or Truth of God. Later on, when Our Blessed Lord promised to give His Body and Blood under the appearance of bread and wine, He implied that He must first ascend to heaven before the Spirit would be given.

He began telling them that His death would happen on the following day; they would see Him no longer with the eyes of the flesh. A little more time must pass, that is to say, the interval between His death and His Resurrection when they would see Him glorified with their bodily eyes. His loss, He assured them, would be compensated for by a greater blessing than His presence in the flesh. The Apostles could not understand what He was saying about the short interval between His death and Resurrection during which their eyes were to be dimmed.

He knew that they were eager to question Him further on this point. Their sorrow and wonderment was not just because He said that He was about to leave them, but also because of the disappointment of their hopes, for they had looked to the establishment of some kind of an earthly kingdom. He assured them that while they were presently case down with grief, the hour would be very brief, just long enough for Him to prove His power over death and to go to His Father. When He passed into the Hour, they would be sad, while His enemies or the world would rejoice. The world would believe that it had done away with Him forever. The grief of His chosen ones, however, would be transitory, for the Cross must become the Crown.

The Cross-pangs are precursors of Resurrection-joys. There must be fellowship with His sufferings before there can be fellowship with His glory. At present, they had sadness because they would no longer see Him in the flesh, but their joy would come through a spiritual quickening, and that joy would have a permanent character about it which the world could not take away.

The nature of this ultimate joy that was to be theirs, the Savior explained in terms of the Comforter, or Paraclete, whom He would send. There would be another Comforter, or "Another to befriend them." "Another" is not a difference in quality, but rather a distinction of persons. He had been their Comforter; He was at their side; He had been One with them and in His Presence they had gained strength and courage; but their trouble was that He was going. He now promised them another Comforter and Advocate. As He would be the Advocate with God in heaven, so the Spirit dwelling within them would plead the cause of God on earth as their Advocate. The Divine secret that He gave was that their loss would now have the greater blessing of the coming of the Spirit. In the Spirit, the Father and the Son would send forth a Divine Power Who would dwell within them and make of their bodies a temple.

The indwelling of the Spirit would mean more than His physical presence among them. So long as Our Lord was with them on earth, His influence was from without inward; but when He would send the Spirit, His influence would radiate from within outward; those who possessed it would have the Spirit of Christ Jesus on earth.

The Holy Spirit would reveal to men the true nature of the great drama that was consummated on the Cross.

"If you love Me you will obey my commands, and I will ask the Father and he will give you another to be your Advocate, who will be with you forever - the Spirit of Truth." (John 14:15, 16)

Quote: *Life of Christ* by **Fulton J. Sheen**
Doubleday Publishing, New York, 1958 edition, pages. 301, 302, 303

Bibliography

The Dolorous Passion of Our Lord Jesus Christ,
   Anne Catherine Emmerich
   Tan Books and Publishers, Inc. Rockford, Illinois, 1983,
   pages. 278, 280-281, 287,

Catherine of Siena, The Dialogue,
   Suzanne Noffke, O.P.
   Paulist Press, New York, 1980, pages.29-30

English Omnibus of the Sources for the Life of St. Francis,
   St. Bonaventure
   Franciscan Press Quincy College, Quincy, Illinois, 1972,
   pages. 821-823

Diary of St. M. Faustina Kowalska,
   St. M. Faustina Kowalska
   Marians of the Immaculate Conception, Stockbridge, Mass.,
   pages. 456-457

The Life and Revelations of St. Gertrude, The Great,
   St. Gertrude
   Tan Books and Publishers, Inc., Rockford, Illinois, 1987,
   pages. 374-376

The Sanctifier,
   Most. Rev. Luis M. Martinez
   Pauline Books and Media, Boston, Mass., 1985, pages. 103-104

I Believe In Love,
   Pere Jean du Coeur Jesus D'Elbee
   St. Bedes' Publications, Petersham, Mass., pages. 119-120

The Life of Christ,
   Fulton J. Sheen
   Doubleday, New York, 1958, pages. 302-304